Ausperity

Lucy Tobin is personal finance editor at the *London Evening Standard*, where she writes a weekly column, 'How to Save it', filled with money-saving ideas. She was named Business Journalist of the Year at the Santander Media Awards and is a frequent guest on TV shows including BBC Breakfast, Sky News, BBC News 24, Five Live and more. Lucy is the author of three previous books, the most recent of which is *Entrepreneur: How to Start an Online Business*.

lucytobin.com

Find an online directory of all the websites recommended in this book at:

ausperity.com

Ausperity

LIVE THE LIFE
YOU WANT FOR LESS

LUCY TOBIN

HERON
BOOKS

First published in Great Britain in 2013 by

Quercus
55 Baker Street
7th Floor, South Block
London W1U 8EW

A CIP catalogue record for this book is available
from the British Library.

PB ISBN 978 1 78087 768 6
EBOOK ISBN 978 1 78087 769 3

10 9 8 7 6 5 4 3 2

Printed and bound in Great Britain by Clays Ltd, St Ives plc

Acknowledgements

To all my friends and family, thank you for signing for voucher-fuelled living – I hope we're still munching at BOGOF restaurants when we're grey 'n' old! To Susan Watt at Heron Books, thank you for picking up the phone and suggesting a lunch (where we both went for the set menu: ausperity through and through), where this book came to life.

Thank you to Ella, Lily and Dory for providing endless hours of (free) fun, laughter and midnight feasts, and to Howard, for setting up money-saving home with me.

This book is for my parents, Lyn and Philip, for being the best.

Contents

Introduction

This was the moment when I realised I had crossed the line to become a fully-fledged money-saving nerd. It was a Monday morning, and I arrived at work to discover a sheepish-looking colleague waiting for me. Over the weekend, he'd spontaneously bought an old sports car. It had come up for sale locally, price tag a few hundred quid. He'd thought it would be fun to use for the odd weekend break; mostly it would sit in his driveway. But when he went to insure it, the cheapest quotes for the most basic cover of his old banger were £1,800-plus. The fun splurge didn't seem so funny anymore. Would I, he asked, find a cheaper deal for him? He'd pay a cut of his saving. Hard-nosed journalist offering to pay out cash? That's how I knew my reputation for frugality had hit embarrassing heights.

I wasn't always this way. The earnings from my first job – babysitting at £3 an hour for doing the neighbours' kids homework for them – barely made a dent on my pocket so quickly was my cash passed over to my local Woolies for sweets and CDs. Growing up, pocket money went on weekend shopping trips and trips to see friends around the country. Britain was booming, recession was something foreign we learnt about in economics lessons. Savings? Cheap deals? They just weren't on the agenda.

Then I went off to uni and spent three years realising that you could either painfully pass over all your cash for rent, utilities, transport costs and other boring bills, or find imaginative ways to pay the lowest amount possible and have more cash spare for the fun stuff in life. At the same time, Britain's economy gradually started falling down the toilet. So when I graduated, moved back home to my childhood bedroom and spent months looking for work, it turned out the most important thing I had learnt at uni wasn't the inanities of Yeats's transcendentalist streak (Huh? Me too – clean forgotten it) but my winning formula for a cheap supermarket bill. So when I finally moved away from home, my uni textbooks on post-modernism went up on my new Ikea shelves, but it was my self-taught crib notes on how to have the most amazing, action-stuffed weekend without shelling out a single penny that were most often in use.

Nowadays, the economy is even worse – fallen out of the toilet and swirling around somewhere in the drains, maybe. No one knows when – if ever – we'll be back to boom, boom Britain again and we're readjusting the way we live. Frankly, we're all feeling poor. Our wages haven't risen since BlackBerry and Apple were just a nice base for a fruit salad. But the cost of that fruit salad has rocketed – as have our taxes, heating, clothes, pets, driving, water, kids, booze, leaving the house, and paying for the privilege of living there too.

But just because life costs more doesn't mean it has to become rubbish. There's no need for a hair shirt or holiday-less year if you trim costs elsewhere – and you might even enjoy doing it. Treats can stay on the agenda when you're paying less for the boring stuff. That's 'ausperity' – living a prosperous life on an austerity budget. How? Read on.

Whether you're at the supermarket or yearning for a manicure, booking a mini-break or in desperate need of a new laptop, when you spend time working out how to save money, you'll find you can afford far more than you thought you could. You might need to devote an extra twenty minutes to booking that week for four in Tenerife or Tallinn, but it will be worth it if doing so saves you £200. You might need to spend the first five minutes of your working day tapping into a train refund site now and then, but if doing so means a tenner back from your delayed commute, the savings will soon tot up, to be spent on something far more fun than just another 07.09 into Birmingham.

Unless you're really living on the breadline, you probably haven't cut back everywhere. I snip off the ends of Colgate tubes to squeeze out an extra few days' toothpaste and mix old lipsticks with Vaseline to make them last longer, but still spend hundreds of pounds a year running my car, which, living in London, I could, if I really, really wanted to, live without. But ausperity living is all about making your own choices; saving money where you want, and making more when you can, to whatever extent you fancy. When I find myself with some spare time at work or in the evenings with a computer and internet available, I make money or earn shopping vouchers by filling in online surveys and joining focus groups. Pretty easy to do in front of the TV – and doing enough each year pays for far more than the TV licence.

Fun, free and cheap days and nights out are all covered in this book, as are ways to raise some quick cash without an *EastEnders*-style trip to a pawn shop. One way is to just rent out your stuff: for example, if little Josh isn't playing with that cello he and his school forced you to fork out for, why not earn £20 a month if someone else's little Josh wants to try it out? And if you've found something you'd love to buy but can't afford it until there's been a hefty discount, visit an online sales-logger. No idea what the dove's doo-dah that is? You soon will. If you're confused about the big stuff – credit cards, mortgages, or budgeting – that's all here too; the high-tech route and the stub-of-pencil-and-paper path, explained in easy, non-boring gobbets which will make it surmountable once more.

Likewise, when I began preparing for my wedding and needed (OK, wanted, after reading too many bridal magazines) to find favours that were cheap but still thoughtful, I spent a few months going through people's recycling bins to accumulate a hundred-odd tin cans, scrubbed them clean, jabbed some draining holes in the bottom, secured some free cuttings of lavender and wrapped them with home-made labels. Sound bonkers and far too time-consuming? I think by the end of six months spent watching over these lavenders like new-borns, I might agree with you. But the best thing about the money-saving and money-making ideas in this book is that you can pick'n'mix. And keeping up the analogy, some ideas will be as easy as jelly babies from that pick'n'mix, others will require a bit of organisation – like a gobstopper: you only start on one when you know you've got some time. Some will instantly save you hundreds of pounds, a few may seem like a bit too much effort for now. Start at whatever level you want, and work your way up. You'll soon be an auspericist.

This book contains money-saving ideas and tips from experts across myriad sectors – from beauticians and car-buyers to interiors experts and ordinary people who have revealed the ways they make and save cash, plus me. As a personal finance journalist I have written thousands of words each month for a 'How to Save it' column for the *Evening Standard*, filled with tiny ideas that tot up to big savings. But most of all, this book comes from my own life: imaginative ways my family, friends and I have worked out how to cut costs as the economy has become gloomier and gloomier.

Together these ideas and advice knock thousands of pounds off the cost of living. It's less shiver-me-timbers-I-can't-afford-to-put-the-heating-on, more ten-easy-tips-to-slash-your-heating-bill-by-a-third. You might not want – or be able – to do everything in this book; you might dip in or out whilst on the loo (I'm not ashamed: some of my best-read books are loo books); or you might (I hope) read it in one bum-numbingly long session that sees you change your money-mindedness forever. Either way, there are a lot of ideas and advice that will start to change the state of your finances, whilst making your lifestyle just as – or even more – enjoyable, very quickly.

So, back to the beginning. You've got less coming in, but deal with it properly and you won't need to sit at home listlessly or turn into Mr or Mrs Boring-on-a-Budget. This book lays out how to save carefully and spend wisely – so you can squeeze more value out of your hard-earned cash and keep on living the high life on a low budget. Enjoy ausperity living.

PART 1
Spending it

IT MIGHT SOUND WEIRD to start a money-saving book by talking about spending it. But that's the point about ausperity: despite our frozen wages, awkwardly combined with rising household costs, we still want to have nice clothes, fun nights out and time with friends. Sometimes we still need – or want – to splurge on big items like a new car or oven. So the next few chapters are all about getting what we want for less.

In fact, in the middle of writing the last sentence I received a 'daily deals' email from Living Social, one of the group-buying sites that works in the same way as Groupon (see page 24 for more details.) I get these every day, and mostly click 'delete'. But this one was offering two meals for £15 plus wine at a particular local restaurant that my family visits on special occasions. Since a main course is usually £7 or £8 and I knew a birthday trip was coming up, I clicked on the deal, checked out the terms and conditions (it worked on the weekend and several could be purchased for one table) and bought it. The site has a recommendation scheme too – you buy the deal, and if three others buy it from your link, your costs are refunded. So I've just emailed the link to my family, posted it on Facebook for my friends and tweeted it for anyone else who lives locally. Hopefully within a few hours I'll have secured my dinner for free.

That's spending it, ausperity-style: clever ways to buy splurge items for less. When they say the best things in life are free, I think that's supposed to mean love, sloppy kisses from a grandchild and stuff like that. But in my experience, it can be true of real-life experiences too. It's easy to secure a great night out that, unlike the ever-rising cost of a trip to the flicks (although you'll find tips here on cutting the cost of that too), won't demand you pay a penny. And you enjoy it more that way, too.

Often, it's about using a bit of imagination (but if that word has filled you with fear, don't worry – you can just copy the ideas in this book) to easily cut down on how much you're spending on extras and luxuries, even whilst often buying or experiencing exactly the same things. One of my most memorable dates, for example, had nothing in common with the conventional (and expensive) dinner out; instead, I was invited to watch a TV show being shot. It was for one of those Saturday morning music shows that no longer exists, and I must admit to feeling less excited when I discovered we'd have to turn up at the studios at 8 a.m. on the first morning of the weekend. But watching the show was so much fun that we went back a few more times (I'm not sure that dates two and three would ever have happened otherwise) and I didn't even think about the fact that the boy hadn't had to pay a penny for the date. By contrast, like most ausperity girls with double standards, I still reckon taking a two-for-one dinner voucher on a date could be a bit of a turn-off . . .

So think about what you do when you need to buy something. If you enjoy shopping, you'll probably block out an afternoon or weekend to browse the shops, try things on or test them out, and buy the one you like best. If you hate shopping, you'll go to the nearest retailer or go online and buy it so quickly your spell of shopping-related nausea barely registers. Either way, you usually know what kind of things you want to buy, or what shop you're going to buy from, and in all cases, a bit of research will save you cash.

This section of *Ausperity* covers everything from cheap and free things to do with kids and on nights out, to bargainous ideas for Christmas, weddings and festivals, and a whopping, massive chunk on holidays. The latter was entirely inspired by my time at uni. I went to a university whose terms only lasted eight weeks. This meant that for three years I had six months of the year free.

For most of them, I worked. For a bit of them, I studied. But I also spent an embarrassing amount of that time working out how to make the most of my earnings in the most fabulous way possible. Back in the golden era of uni vacations, I could easily spend two weeks solidly focused on booking a holiday – which meant nabbing the best possible deals and learning all the tricks of the tourism trade. A few months after our final exams, a boyfriend and I took a trip to Chicago, Costa Rica, Miami and New York. We had spent three months working to pay for it, we had three weeks to play with and we wanted a bit of luxury. Still, nobody we subsequently bored with our 400 holiday snaps could believe that we visited eight different destinations, took six flights, stayed in eleven different four-star hotels, enjoyed great cuisine, paid for all transfers, lots of bags of shopping and travel insurance – for £1,000 each.

How did we do it? By finding bargain-bucket flights (see page 82), researching free attractions (including Chicago's amazing zoo) and printing money-off vouchers to get into galleries and museums before we left. We had picked our destinations based on the positive exchange rate, and made savings on things that didn't matter – so transfers often involved minibus journeys where the seats felt like a bucking bronco's saddle, but that was OK for an hour if it meant a nicer hotel was affordable at the end. We went in the rainy season, having researched that what that really meant was an hour's serious rain per day and much, much cheaper hotels.

This won't always be the case – I'd give the Caribbean a miss in hurricane season even if the hotels were paying me – but if, in these straitened times, you might think a holiday is out of the question this year, or maybe your usual two or three breaks is to be trimmed down to one, don't assume that's true – instead, read pages 67–103. Perhaps you'll find yourself reading the other chapters whilst leaving, on a jet plane . . .

Shopping

I love shopping. Sometimes there's nothing more fun than an afternoon hitting the shops, checking out what's new, snapping up bargains or 'investments' (aka really desirable shoes). I have to get that in now in case you soon think I sound completely sackcloth. I'm not – my wardrobe is chock-a-block and every room of my flat shows evidence of my love of shopping. Being a penny-pincher doesn't have to mean never buying new clothes or furniture or trinkets or whatever floats your personal materialism boat. It just means shopping cleverly – beating the retailers at their own money-making game – and paying the lowest possible price and/or getting the best possible value. Whether you prefer the bricks-and-mortar shops on the high street or take your mouse for a walk in e-tail, follow the steps below and savvy shopping will soon become second nature. And if it seems tedious at first, just think of all the extra treats you can buy with the money you're saving . . .

On the high street

If you're buying something expensive or from a brand name, it's worth doing some online research first to work out what kind of price you should be paying. Often the high street shopping experience is much better than the internet: you can try stuff on, see how it actually looks and feels, and receive advice from assistants who might even know what they're talking about. Local, independent shops often have really unusual designs that you won't find anywhere else, and if you want them to stay alive and open when you *really* need that birthday present for Dad that you forgot to buy until the evening of his sixtieth birthday, then you need to patronise them. Price research is still crucial though – you should know whether you're paying a fair price (remember online shopping usually involves postage costs which aren't added until the checkout), and sometimes high street stores will throw in extras such as gift wrap, a free extended guarantee or something like a packet of batteries or a refill pack that goes with the product.

Once you're out and about, smartphones offer an easy way to price-check. Either look up the name of the product in a comparison site like kelkoo.co.uk, pricerunner.co.uk or Google Shopping, or use a free app like RedLaser, which allows you to scan in barcodes on goods you want to buy in shops, and will then check to see if they are available cheaper online or nearby. Shoparazzi is another useful free app which shows you the latest sales and sample sales at both local boutiques and big chain stores (shoparazzi.com or look it up on your phone's app store) near wherever you are. If possible, use a cashback credit card (see page 231) for all purchases to earn money back from your spending. And join all possible loyalty schemes – not shop credit cards, which typically demand very high interest rates after any offers run out, but points-based reward cards such as Tesco Clubcard, Boots Advantage Card, Nectar, Superdrug Beautycard and so on.

These can tot up to large discounts – in fact, my wallet is bulging with them. I don't even go into Boots very often, but its scheme is generous enough that, every few months or so I find I have at least a chocolate bar's worth of points to use instead of money. Tesco's Clubcard often runs double-reward deals, so never use the points in store: I saved them up for long enough that a few months' worth of onions etc. gave me a family trip to Chessington World of Adventures. Oh, and the Superdrug loyalty card is doubly useful: made of silver, it acts as an emergency mirror.

Ker-ching for checking in

New cashback schemes mean you can even get paid to walk into shops. Not much, natch, but still. iPhone and Android phone owners who download a free Quidco app can, when visiting certain stores, receive between 10p and 50p – and hey, it all adds up, and if you're out shopping anyway . . . The app's GPS technology will also tell you which shops participating in the scheme are near to wherever you are, so you can darken their door and scoop up the money. Shops involved include Carphone Warehouse (25p for passing its threshold), B&Q (20p) and Mountain Warehouse (20p). The app also has vouchers for money-off spending and cashback when you're in various stores.

If you're out and spot a piece of clothing that you love but can't afford, it's worth logging it into lovefashionsales.com once you're home. The site is free, and will send you an email alert every time your favourite shop starts a sale or cuts prices on items in your size. You can set up alerts that are as wide ('Banana Republic') or as narrow ('Banana Republic tops, size eight') as you like. The site includes 8,000 British shops and brands.

More discounts

You might think that taking a student on a shopping trip would only be a drain on your wallet, but not so: thousands of shops offer student discounts of ten per cent or more, so grabbing a uni-goer may be worthwhile, especially for expensive shopping sprees. They can be especially useful for computing discounts – the latest Microsoft Office software package costs over £100, but is available for just over £30 to anyone with an 'ac.uk' email address – so that's school kids, university students or teachers – via software company Viglen (http://viglen.software2.co.uk). There are big student discounts on 'i' stuff too: Apple takes between ten per cent and fourteen per cent off most of its products for students.

'Always ask for a discount in any non-chain shop – you never know what you'll get, and in my experience, there's always a deal to be done.' – SIMONE, LONDON

It's worth checking out charity shops for great deals too – especially those on the posher side of town where the best donations are likely to be made. My fiancé never buys DVDs from the high street or even cheap online deals, but instead buys them for £1 or £2 from charity shops, and if they're so bad we don't want to watch them again, the DVDs go straight back again. In London, *Time Out* has a list of its favourite charity shops at tinyurl.com/ timeoutcharityshops.

'Get a loyalty card for whatever places you shop or eat out at the most.'
— *DAN, LONDON*

Try car boot sales (carbootjunction.com and carbootsrus. com list hundreds), or if you're not a fan of early mornings, summer fêtes at schools and churches (look out for those in the smartest neighbourhoods for the best finds) can also yield clothing bonanzas. And don't forget discount stores. TK Maxx, for example, sells what it calls 'designer labels for less'. Some of its rails are a mess but get there early and be patient and you could find a bargain, be it a £5 Nike hoody for exercising in (I always buy my sweaty gear from there at a fraction of the price elsewhere), a ball gown for a wedding or a designer handbag (excellent deals, and arranged by colour, which is particularly helpful!). TK Maxx also sells perfume and cosmetics by beauty brands like Clinique and Clarins, whilst bigger branches host homeware and toy sections, with cheap bedding, cushions and playthings that make excellent you'd-never-guess-the-price presents.

Outlets

Designer outlet villages and factory shops can also offer big bargains. Amongst the best-known are:

- **The McArthur Glen chain** (with six across the UK including Ashford, East Midlands, Cheshire Oaks, Swindon and York, and shops including Diesel, Timberland, Adidas, Lacoste, Burberry and Prada).

- **The Bicester Village Outlet** near Oxford (with brands including Molton Brown, SuperDry, Donna Karan, Jigsaw and Le Crueset). This is my (relatively) local. Get there early to avoid the crowds, and take some grub with you because the food options are limited to posh and packed or Pret A Manger.

- **Clarks Village** in Somerset (with Gap, Jane Shilton, Next, Monsoon and Marks & Spencer).

Online shopping

If you know exactly what you want, it's very easy to find the best price online. The first step is to embrace cashback websites. These sites pay you when you click on to certain websites or buy something from thousands of retailers. They pass on the commission they get from the shops and are either free or take an annual fee out of your earnings (so if you don't use them, you don't pay). I don't think of myself as a big online shopper, but even so I've earned £1,300 in my past four years as a member of cashback site Quidco.

Cashback

Feeling suspicious about cashback? No surprise – it does feel like something for nothing, and even the industry admits that, as Jo Roberts of Quidco puts it, 'despite millions of online shoppers recognising the benefits of using third-party websites, many remain in the dark about how they actually work.' So I asked her to explain. 'Retailers pay a commission each time a customer completes a transaction having clicked from a cashback website. This entire commission, paid by the retailer to the cashback site, is then returned to the shopper's bank account in the form of cashback. It is that simple.'

Downloading a free 'cashback reminder' toolbar for your web browser or an app for your mobile is another way to secure savings. 'Referring friends and family is another great means of topping up your cashback accounts,' Roberts adds. 'Always eager to expand their memberships, all the top sites offer financial incentives for those who introduce new people to their services. In some cases, fees up to £5 are available.'

The money-saving steps to online shopping:

1. **Log into a cashback site.** Take your pick: the biggest include topcashback.co.uk, quidco.com and greasypalm.co.uk.

2. **Use it to click through to a price-comparison site**, such as kelkoo.co.uk or priceinspector.co.uk and search for your item. There are also specialist comparison services, such as fragrancescompared.co.uk to find discounts on particular perfumes.

3. **Once you've found the item you want to buy,** at the cheapest price available from a site with good reviews and recommendations and that you trust, look online for a discount voucher. You can find these collated in one place via a site like myvouchercodes.co.uk – where you can search via store or shopping category – or just Google the name of the product you want to buy or shop you want to buy it from, together with the phrase 'discount code' or 'voucher code'.

4. **Delete your computer's cookies** – these are like footprints in the sand proving you've previously been at the website – to boost your chances of receiving cashback. You need the cashback company to think you've not been to the shop's website before, so click to clear your cookies to wipe away your earlier trail.

   To do so in Internet Explorer, just close all your internet windows. Open IE again, click 'tools', then 'general options', then 'delete cookies'. Click 'OK' and close the window.

   On Mozilla Firefox, click the 'tools' menu on an internet window, select 'options' and 'privacy', and on the 'keep cookies' option click 'until I close Firefox', which will wipe them every time you close down your browser.

   Or on Google Chrome, click the spanner button, then 'options', then the 'under the bonnet' tab, and 'clear browsing data'.

5. **Once that's completed, return to the cashback site** and click on the link to your shopping website. The sites include most of the biggest brands like Tesco, BT, Sky, Netflix, Gap and Debenhams, as well as online-only stores.

These steps might sound complicated, but they will quickly become part of your online shopping routine – just like taking your purse when hitting the shops – and help save you a fortune.

A caveat on cashback

Different sites offer cashback at different websites, so for the really keen, it's worth signing up with several sites. There's an easy way to search which provider offers the most cashback for a particular site: visit tinyurl.com/cashbacksites. Look out for minimum payments on some sites, which won't pay out until you've earned a minimum fee, and don't let cashback offers blind you to the price you're actually paying. Earning ten per cent back from, say, photo development site Truprint could still work out more expensive if its basic prices are more expensive than another site's. Be aware that discount codes sometimes cancel out cashback, so if you're using the former be aware that your cashback claim might be invalidated – never count on having the money until it's actually paid, which can take up to three months.

More online money-saving shopping tips

Some shops never, or rarely, get involved in discounts or cashback, and one of those is one of the biggest on the web: Amazon. But there's an easy way to track down bargains from Amazon's vast store of books, music, furnishings and now even groceries: sign up to zeezaw.co.uk, type in the items that you want to buy and the price you want to pay. The site will then watch the products on Amazon on your behalf and ping you an email when they go on sale at the price you want. For more general bargains, pricecutreview. com/uk lists the Amazon items that are on sale at fifty per cent off or more.

There are student discounts online, too: students who have a current National Union of Students Extra Card, for example, receive a ten per cent discount on clothing and a five per cent discount on books, music, DVDs and everything else sold on Amazon.

If you're a keen eBay shopper, it's worth checking out fatfingers.co.uk. Type in whatever you're hoping to bid for, and the site will search the giant auctions site for similar listings that incorporate common typos, so you uncover items that others aren't finding because they are spelt wrong and therefore have low or no bids. It's worth also using a 'sniper' such as auctionstealer.co.uk, which allows you to automatically place bids at the last possible moment before the sale closes, giving you a better chance of winning the bid at a low price – and meaning you don't have to sit in front of a computer watching bids for hours.

Be wary of sales: always do some shopping maths before you splash out. That reduced T-shirt that costs only

£10 won't be a good deal if you wear it once, realise lime green and orange just isn't your colour combination and that perhaps there was a reason it was the only thing left on the sales rack, and chuck it out. By contrast, a really warm winter coat that's more expensive, but better quality, than what you usually buy could well be a worthwhile purchase if it lasts years – remember to think about the cost per wear, not just the outright cost, when buying anything.

'I always try clothes on before the sales start, so that when they do kick off, I already know what I want to buy, and don't have to faff about in cramped changing rooms but can get straight to the till with my bargain.'
— *SUSAN, NORTH LONDON*

And if you fall in love with an expensive item of clothing or piece of furniture or anything else pricey that you just can't justify buying, think about sharing it. If you and a good friend both love the same thing, is it possible (and practical) to go halves on it and each use it half of the time? Be wary of doing so with anyone but a very good friend who you trust and can get along with well enough to share properly.

Group-buying

These sites were one of the fastest growing website ideas to come out of the recession. If you've ever seen an advert or had an email pop into your inbox promising a day at a spa for £20, dinner for two for £15 (the deal I bought and wrote about earlier), a photo book for a fiver, a three-night holiday in Majorca for £150 or five sessions of colonic irrigation (this pops up with alarming frequency) for the price of three, that's group buying. There are loads of sites, and each offers something slightly different, but the idea is the same: shops, websites and services know they can still make a profit on reduced items if they can guarantee a certain level of interest. So they agree deals with a site like Groupon, promising a reduced-price experience or purchase. Sometimes there are tipping points – the deal is only 'released' when a specific number of people sign up – but sometimes it's a free-for-all. The deals all run out at a specific time or when a particular number have been bought.

Sometimes the sites offer amazing deals. I've snapped up a £15 Marks & Spencer voucher from livingsocial.com for £7. Given that I needed some new PJs and was going to head to M&S anyway, I saved more than half price. In fact, I saved even more than that, because Living Social, in common with a lot of its rivals, offers the deal free if you can convince three friends to sign up. I just posted my referral link on Twitter and Facebook and quickly secured more than the required number of sign-ups.

But group-buying deals are not always what they seem. I recently bought a Bluetooth headset from another group-buying site, which claimed the car phone set was worth £80, so paying £20 seemed worthwhile. Alas, it wasn't even worth that – it took over six weeks to arrive, and when it did it was clunky, slow and poor quality. I wished I'd stuck with a traditional retailer. So the golden rule with group buying deals is, as with all shopping, only buy it if you need it or would buy it anyway at full price.

Plus, one thing I've never seen a group-discounts site offer is a reduced eye test – and that could be because they don't want us to be very good at reading small print. Most group-buying vouchers have acres of fine print, with restrictions on when you can redeem the voucher, how long they last, the number and nature of people who can get involved – and so on. A lot of spa deals, for example, can only be redeemed midweek. And restaurant or bar deals will rarely be offered at peak times. Nick Telson, from money-saving nightlife website designmynight.com, advises: 'Venues use deals to help fill their sites during quieter periods, they do not need hundreds of people in on discounts on the weekend. So you must do your research into the venue before you buy a deal.

'Check out the restaurant's own website closely and especially look at its price lists. If you have a restaurant deal with fifty per cent off food, it is more than likely that the restaurant will be looking to make their money back on alcohol. Does the restaurant have a specific wine list available to deal users only? What is the cheapest bottle of wine on the wine list? It would be a disaster to enjoy a wonderful discount on food and then get hit with a £30-a-bottle wine purchase on the bill.

And make a note of the deal you have bought and when it expires. It is so easy to buy a fantastic deal and see that it expires a few months from the purchase date. So you save it in your inbox and then . . . completely forget about it. That's just a waste of money. Put a reminder in your diary a few weeks before the expiry date to ensure that you use it. If you do all of the above, then using deal and voucher sites is a very effective way to go out on a budget. Oh, and don't be scared to ask for a jug of tap water . . . venues must legally provide water for all paying customers!'

The biggest group-buying sites

- **Groupon.co.uk** – nationwide deals. A lot of medical treatments like physio and dentist deals, plus spa breaks and holidays. Other samples include a large bean bag for £39, down from £149, and a two-piece suit for £79 rather than £249. Has a tipping point plus a 'recommend a friend' scheme, where users receive £6 for every friend brought on board who buys a deal within seventy-two hours of referral. Can sign up for city-specific deals.

- **Wowcher.com** – nationwide deals. Has a large range of offers, from car-driving days (sample offers: three-day Porsche driving experience for £490 rather than £1,282, London bus tour ticket for £8 not £16). Money only taken out of your account once a tipping point is reached.

- **Kelkooselect.co.uk** – nationwide, but often London-focused. I've found fewer offers than on the above sites, but recent ones have included £29 for ten hour-long boot camp fitness sessions at a central London gym, discounted photo canvasses and West End musical tickets.

- **Keynoir.com** – has deals around the country, but again many are in London. They include cupcake decorating classes (£27 rather than £55), and champagne afternoon tea at a West End hotel (£38 for two rather than £59). Pays out either a refund on your deal or a credit (depending on offer) when friends sign up.

- **Livingsocial.com** – different versions for different cities, including London broken up into north, south-east, south-west, and east. Link in three people to buy the deal you buy and it's free. Recent deals include three cookbooks from the Leon restaurant chain for £27 – a fifty per cent saving – and a haircut for £39 rather than £80.

- **Wahanda.com** – specialises in health and beauty, including facials, mani/pedicures, massages and spa breaks. Recent offers have included a 'Moroccan ritual' spa day for two at the May Fair Hotel in central London for £69. Recommending a friend will give them £5 off their first purchase and you gain a £5 discount once the friend has bought a deal.

Nightlife

You're having a big night out on the town. You leave the house, taking just one card ('for emergencies,' you tell yourself) and a £20 note to spend on the evening. It's just a light night, a couple of friends and a few drinks, home not too late, got lots to do tomorrow. Well, that's the plan. But that never happens. The reality? It's 2 p.m. on Sunday, you've woken up with that horrible feeling in your mouth, throat, stomach – and worst of all, head – and your credit card looks a lot more worn than it did the night before. Nightlife economics don't always work out how you expect.

But there are loads of ways to enjoy a night out without spending a bomb – and some free ideas are even exciting enough to wow a first date. Who wouldn't be impressed by tickets to a prime-time TV show, for example? Or a tiny private gig or theatre tickets that no one but you knows cost only a tenner?

Bars and clubs

When you're going out boozing, some expenses just can't be avoided. If a friend has booked a London bar for a birthday that charges £10 entry, you can hardly stand outside chatting to your mates through the toilet window to avoid the door fee. But you can try to convince said friend to host the big night in a free spot – or, even better, one with drinks deals or free entertainment. But where to go? In London, you can follow the advice of Nick Telson again, who, whilst researching his nightlife comparison site designmynight.com, spent the past two years visiting thousands of pubs, clubs and bars to build a database where you can search for nightlife via area, cost or type of venue. That way, you'll know in advance exactly how much passing the threshold of a bar or club will set you back, and the cost of every cocktail or pint thereafter. There are also deals, with Groupon-style bulk-buying discounts where spending, say, £15 provides £30 worth of food or drink at particular spots around town. Plus the site offers a free concierge service, where its founders will help you plan a night out in London – whether it's a birthday bash or corporate do where you need to impress the boss on the cheap – without going over-budget.

'Drink tap water with your meal when out in a restaurant. Soft drinks like Coke are sometimes as expensive as the food. And don't get me started on the cost of the hard stuff.' – MORAY, EDINBURGH

Outside of the capital, the duo's bar-browsing experiences have given them a wealth of knowledge about economising on a night out. Here are Telson and Webster's top tips:

- **Save on transport** – pre-book cabs at home before you go out so you can search for the best prices and don't pay over the odds outside a club, where cab firms can often have a monopoly and overcharge you. Alternatively, plan ahead and write down your night bus route so you know how to get home and won't have to pay for a cab.

- **Time your arrival** – many top bars and clubs will tier their entry-price levels, so get to the venue as early as you can. Many are free before 8 p.m. and then rise in price every hour. If you get into a bar early it is more than likely that there will be a promotion or happy hour too. The cost you save having pre drinks at home will normally come back to bite you on later entry fees and full-price drinks in the bar or club.

- **Book in advance** – times have changed: nowadays, when going to top bars and nightclubs, you should book as if you were going to a restaurant. Not only will this guarantee you entry but you can bargain with the venue, asking them to give you a drinks deal on arrival and reduced guest-list prices. If you just show up and want to get in, you have less bargaining power.

- **Don't do rounds** – if you are a light drinker do not get pulled into doing rounds with your friends! This will end up with you having to buy a huge amount for everyone when normally you can get by on just a couple of drinks.

- **Be spirit-savvy** – if you see mixologists heading for the top-shelf spirit when making your drink you can always enquire into what the house spirit is and whether this will make the drink cheaper. If a bar is pouring you a spirit and mixer with their most expensive spirit then the likelihood is that the final drink will also be more expensive. It never hurts to ask!

- **Happy Hours** – with the advent of deals sites, people seem to have forgotten about happy hours. But they still exist and are actually becoming more and more prevalent as venues need to fill their establishments during this tough economic climate. You will now find that even the most luxurious bars will have an early doors happy hour to lure you in after work. They are a great way of discovering the best nightlife a city has to offer at half the price.

- **Keep your eye on the clock** – if you are in a bar with a happy hour or special promotion, do not be afraid to buy a couple of rounds in at once before the deal ends. This can keep you going in the bar for a few hours longer without having to pay again (at the more expensive prices).

- **Check prices before going out** – always look online to find out the prices of drinks before you set off. You may be attracted by the latest cool bar that has rave reviews only to realise when you get there that cocktails cost £12 a go. If you spend five minutes checking before you set off you won't have any nasty surprises when you arrive.

- **Don't feel embarrassed** – the English nature is never to say no. When in a restaurant or a bar where there is table service, the waiter or host will be constantly topping up your drink and then asking if you would like another one. It is OK to say no! If you have already ordered and enjoyed one expensive cocktail or a bottle of wine, it is then OK to enjoy the surroundings and atmosphere of the bar without having to have a drink on your table. There is no law that says you must always have a drink to hand if you are in a bar or restaurant.

Staying in – party for five. Or fifty . . .

Nowadays a night out in town tends to involve doing battle with cab drivers or parking restrictions, queuing to get in, being unhappily forced to then pay more again for the privilege of not wearing your winter coat, paying over the odds – albeit less so with the above tips – for drinks, then having to repeat the last step three times to get out of the grumpy mood steps one, two and three have put you in. Or maybe that's just me. Celebratory nights out in restaurants can equally be spoiled by the noise of other peoples' kids screaming or the stress of splitting the bill when stingy Sophie in the corner underpays or no one puts in for a tip . . . Little surprise so many of us are now opting to celebrate birthdays and other events by throwing parties at home. These are almost always better than their café/club/professional equivalent – and they don't have to cost a bomb.

At my engagement party last year, we hosted seventy people and, given the one-off nature of the occasion and large number of guests, expected the bill to be hefty. In fact, not only was it pretty reasonable, but it was so much fun that we've pledged to throw a big party every year.

The main costs were food and booze, but once we'd price-compared it all on mysupermarket.com, we found we could stock up on all the essentials quite reasonably – and you'd be amazed how professional a load of pitta bread, houmous, a few other dips and 300 homemade mushroom vol-au-vents look.

You can also host a dinner party with a twist, by asking everyone to bring a dish. My parents have been doing these with the same group of friends for at least two decades and they have barely replicated a theme yet. The host names the theme – Italian night, American, taco dinner, fondue, camping (hot dogs, s'mores etc.), fish and chips, Thai, Chinese, barbecue, sushi, curry, etc. – and everyone sends an 'email all' around saying what they will contribute, as well as bringing a bottle. The host then just has to offer their table and their washing-up facilities.

Other fun, and low-cost, party ideas include afternoon tea – bake some scones (see page 136) and a cake, set up a dish of tangerines or grapes or other fruit, boil the kettle, and you're off. Board games night always goes down well with my friends: not so much Scrabble, but big group games like Articulate (split into teams who have to guess what's being described); charades (act out a film, book or TV show); or my favourite, of which I've no idea if it has a proper name, but involves everyone sticking a Post-it note on their nearest neighbour's head with a well-known person's name on – they then have to guess who it is, twenty-questions style.

Theatre and sports tickets

Nights (or days) out at the theatre, concerts or big sporting or arts events can often cost a fortune. The face-value ticket price at most major events is usually already high, then agencies add on booking fees, card payment charges, maybe ticket postage costs too, and the price rockets. So if you know exactly what ticket you want, your ambition should be to get it at face value or less – which will involve avoiding the pricey booking fees that both promoters and agencies slap on to tickets. You can do so by visiting the box office (or stadium for a sporting event, gallery for a blockbuster arts event) if it's near enough. Usually – although, unbelievably, not always – doing so will allow you to avoid postage costs. Or phone the venue's ticket hotline. This will usually be slightly pricier, but going via an agency will usually cost even more. If tickets have sold out, or are too expensive, it's worth looking elsewhere, such as via a comparison site or ticket exchange website. The biggest agencies include Ticketmaster (ticketmaster. co.uk), Ticketline (ticketline.co.uk) and Star Green (stargreen.com), but unfortunately all will hit you with fees. Comparison sites that will help you shop around include comparetheatretickets.com, seatchoice.com and theatrebillboard.com, whilst theatremonkey.com lists hundreds of theatre and music deals in London.

Other ticket-buying sites such as viagogo.co.uk and seatwave.com were set up for fans to sell on tickets to events that they can no longer go to. It's worth checking the sites out for prices and availability, but take care to ensure that the ticket you buy is genuine. The same is true for any bought off classified websites like gumtree.com and eBay. If you do opt to buy from another individual, especially online, ask for proof of purchase, such as a card payment receipt or official emailed receipt, and information about the seller, such as a landline phone number, address and/or work email. Explain why you are keen to secure the information – if they are reluctant to give it, you might want to reconsider the purchase.

Other ways to bag a ticket bargain include scouting around lastminute.com's deals – some include tickets for a tenner, especially at regional theatres around the country. In London, Shakespeare's Globe offers 700 tickets for £5 each at every performance – you do have to stand up, but you'll have the best view of the stage. Likewise, the National Theatre in London releases £5 standing tickets on the days of sold-out performances. I once went to see Alan Bennett's *The History Boys* for a fiver with a friend this way – and after spotting some empty seats in the stalls, the usher let us slink into them at the interval.

For other West End shows, you can get cheaper tickets for performances on the day of your visit at the Half Price TKTS Booth in Leicester Square and in Brent Cross shopping centre, north London. Each morning, theatres send over tickets for leftover seats for that day, and you can check online at tkts.co.uk before trekking to the booth. In Leicester Square, make sure you visit the official booth, run by the Society of London Theatre, rather than the lookalike agencies which may charge higher prices, or touts whose tickets may not even be genuine.

Students, seniors and unemployed people can often secure a discounted ticket at theatres by asking at the box office a few hours before the performance begins. Hunt out niche performances at local drama colleges and am-dram societies – some will be awful, some will be amazing, but looking out for reviews in blogs and local papers will help you to cherry-pick the best.

Kicking up a fuss

The same is true for sports events: the Champion's League final is always going to be a sell out, but Barnet vs Gillingham might be available, and have tickets costing less than ten per cent of the cost of a premier league match. Likewise, admission to the Cheltenham Gold Cup may be expensive, but the UK has sixty race courses and they have race days all the time (britishracecourses.org). If you're a big fan of a particular sport or side, the best way to get the most reasonable tickets (let's be honest – unless it's tiddlywinks that you follow, big sports are unlikely to ever be cheap, and reasonable is the best you can hope for) is to join the fan club.

England football supporters get access to tickets via the England fans club (http://englandfans.thefa.com); the Wimbledon tennis championships allocate tickets to local tennis clubs for their members and also hold a ballot for the public between August and December each year (lta.org.uk).

Free live entertainment

I've written earlier about watching a TV show being filmed. It's a free night (or day) out and the shows on offer range enormously, so you're likely to find something that covers your taste. Your main options are going through an agency or direct to the likes of the BBC. Standing Room Only (sroaudiences.com) has shows including *They Think It's All Over*, *Sports Relief*, *Would I Lie to You*, *The Jonathan Ross*

Show and *Mock the Week*. Other sources include Applause Store (applausestore.com), with free tickets including *Britain's Got Talent*, *Million Pound Drop* and *The Magicians*. The BBC offers free audience tickets to loads of its own TV and radio shows and has opportunities to feature on its shows at bbc.co.uk/showsandtours.

Don't forget the brainy kinds of nights out. Major galleries and museums now open late at least once a week and many are free, including the National Portrait Gallery, British Museum, Royal Academy and Tate galleries around the UK. Local colleges and civic centres often host free lectures – keep an eye on a local listings site. *Time Out* is great for the capital – at timeout.com/London – whilst the View sites (the website is 'view' followed by the nameofthetown.co.uk, such as viewbath.co.uk) cover Bath, Belfast, Birmingham, Bournemouth, Bradford, Brighton, Bristol, Cambridge, Cardiff, Edinburgh, Glasgow, Hull, Leeds, Leicester, Liverpool, London, Manchester, Nottingham, Oxford and Sheffield.

Another way to see free live entertainment is by taking advantage of festival volunteering opportunities. Smaller music venues and all of the major music festivals offer opportunities for volunteers to get in for free by spending some of the time working as a steward. The schemes are usually run by charities such as WaterAid, Greenpeace and Oxfam. For the summer festivals, applications usually open between three and six months before the festival is due to take place, so keep an eye on websites such as oxfam.org. uk/stewarding.

Cinema

Has anything seen more price inflation recently than the cinema? I went out with some friends a few weeks ago and our tickets plus the cost of the smallest box of popcorn (which admittedly was almost the size of the average bathroom – I couldn't stop them from buying it) came to almost £50. It was a rare lack of cinema financial planning for us, because if you plan ahead you can shave the cost of a night at the flicks down to the quick. On tickets, work out when is cheapest to go. Cinemas are keen to get just as many bums on seats during off-peak times as over the weekends. So lots of places, including the Cineworld chain, offer cut-price deals midweek, such as on Tuesday nights. Meanwhile, anyone with an Orange mobile phone – or a friend who has one – can get two-for-one cinema tickets every Wednesday. If you've no Orange customers in your circle, just get an Orange sim card for free, then top it up with £5 credit and switch the phone on just on Wednesdays, purely to secure your free ticket (see orange.co.uk/freesim).

Alternatively, anyone who goes to the cinema more than twice a month will usually make savings with an annual membership. The major cinema chains offer these, but so, too, do independents: my local Phoenix art- house cinema charges £25 for a year's membership, which includes two cinema tickets, two discounts on friends' tickets, and £2 off every regular film screening. For movie fans, the savings will quickly become worthwhile.

Or secure free cinema tickets whilst ensuring you're ahead of the crowd by signing up for previews via sites like seefilmfirst.com and Momentum Pictures (momentumpictures.co.uk). You won't want to see every flick they offer (unless you've got the broadest possible taste) but sign up to their email list and invitations to previews at your local cinemas will trickle though.

And once you've got into the cinema, however you got there, steer clear of the concession stand. Insiders admit the profit margin on popcorn is more than 1,200 per cent – a bag of popping corn from the supermarket will cost you 50p per 100 grams, but cinemas charge more than £6 per 100 grams. That's a pretty expensive fee for kernels plus air. Make your own at home, buy a bag from a cheaper source first, bring another snack, or just enjoy the film without munching. But if you do bring some food with you, be careful of the snack-sniffers on the door. My local multiplex has installed a goon on the door to check bags – nominally for security reasons, but when he found my bag of Maltesers and can of Coke, he made me check them in, airport-style, at the ticket desk where they were confiscated until I left the cinema. Ever since, I've carefully hidden my food in the hood of my coat. No one thinks to look . . .

Or create your own cinema night at home, with a borrowed, bought or rented DVD, some popcorn, friends, your sofa and dimmed lights.

'Buy videos, DVDs, books and CDs from charity shops – you can come across some odd little gems and they usually only cost £1 or £2' – GILLIAN, NORTH LONDON

Buying the big stuff

When spending a serious chunk of money – then, more than ever – the key is to think of value rather than just price. Go for items that will last a long time and have a low cost-per-use, not a TV that fatally fizzles out after two years because it was a cheap knock-off, or a second-hand car that shakes when driven above 30 mph and needs major work.

Household appliances

With a big purchase like a new oven or boiler, think price, reliability and running costs. If you have to call out a plumber nine times to fix that 'bargain' washing machine, the maintenance costs will quickly mount up, and likewise a large appetite for power can be very pricey over the life of a white good. A third of every household's energy consumption comes from electrical appliances, according to the Energy Saving Trust (EST). So when it's time to replace one, particularly the most energy-eating devices – kitchen appliances, TVs and other entertainment equipment – look into energy efficiency. New rules mean a device's greenness (or lack of) has to be made clear in an efficiency label. These are comprehensively explained at energylabels.co.uk which will help you know what to look out for.

Energy ratings on appliances are usually based on

size categories, so an example given by the EST is that an A-rated 180-litre fridge freezer could cost only £36 a year to run, whereas a larger 525-litre fridge freezer – even if it had a better A+ rating for efficiency – would still cost more to run, coming in at about £49 a year. If your goggle-box is cinema-sized, your energy bill probably is too. Says the EST: 'The larger a television is, the more energy it will consume, regardless of its energy rating. An A-rated 22-inch LCD TV will typically cost £5 a year to run. An A-rated 56-inch TV would cost £19.' That price difference might not be enough to stop you installing an Odeon-sized megascreen if you find one, but you should still know what you're getting yourself into. Remember to always switch the screen off properly too: homes waste as much as £40 a year leaving things on standby (see page 261 on the Standby Buster).

The EST lists the devices it rates as cheapest to run on its site: tinyurl.com/est-home. If you're thinking of buying a new computer, note that laptops use as much as ninety per cent less electricity each year than their bigger desktop equivalents, slicing about £30 off the average annual energy bill.

For more research on reliability, I rate consumer group Which?'s product reviews. They're only available to members, but you can usually secure a month or two free membership, and if not, anyone making a few big purchases over a year could find paying up worthwhile.

Cars

The quickest way to wipe the value off a new car is to drive it off the forecourt. So goes the joke . . . But unfortunately it's oh-so-true. Traditionally, second-hand cars offer much better value for money. In the current climate, even new-car salesmen are tripping over themselves to secure customers, so it's worth investigating the price difference. However, you're still more likely to drive off with a considerably cheaper deal with 'new to you' rather than 'new'. Either way, it's crucial to learn the tricks of the trade before parting with your cash in the notoriously slippery car-buying industry. So here Phill Jones, commercial director of car-selling site motors.co.uk, offers his ten-point guide to getting the best possible deal on a used car:

1. **Check the basics.** Inspect the bodywork in good light, checking particularly for corrosion or rust. Make sure the brake pedal offers good resistance and doesn't sink most of the way to the floor when applied. Look for rust at the top and rear of the front wings, along the side sills, below front and rear bumpers and the bottom of the doors.

2. **Ensure you're getting good value.** Diesel cars offer fuel efficiency and lower tax rates, and can save families up to £350 a year. Smaller cars often depreciate the least in value over their first year: a Vauxhall Corsa costing £9,475 new, for example, dropped only thirteen per cent to £8,206 in the past twelve months.

3. **Manufacturer warranties and service deals.** These are given away with most new cars (usually lasting three years, though some marques give away more) but can be secured from a used-car sale too if you buy

through a main dealer. These are a good points to haggle over.

4. **Avoid fraud.** Never buy a car without a V5C registration document (logbook). By calling the DVLA on 0300 790 6802 you can check that the car's colour, engine size and date of registration match the V5C. Also ensure that the MOT certificate is valid and see if there were any 'advisories' that may need attention soon, such as worn tyres. Beware of used cars that are sold with a short MOT – the owner may know something you don't. Check how many months of car tax remain on the vehicle. For example, a car with an engine size of 1.5cc or smaller worked out at around £130 per year in 2010/2011.

5. **Haggle.** Mastering it correctly could end up saving thousands on your dream car. How to do it? Well, if buying privately, research similar cars as a comparison point. Try not to seem confused or overwhelmed; being cool and collected is the key. Don't be tricked into buying a higher spec car than you actually need. Start at a low opening price but be realistic. Let the other person negotiate you up to a price you are both happy with. Deliver an ultimatum. If you are getting close to a deal, say that you will buy a particular car at a particular price – if they agree now. Don't be afraid to walk away if you're not a hundred per cent sure. There is always another car and another deal.

6. **Technology.** This has really taken off in recent years; you can even tweet via your steering wheel. Be realistic about the extras you really need. Having a hands-free

kit makes a car more appealing to buy, especially with British road laws strictly enforcing the use of phones when driving. But you can fit your own for as little as £50. If you're looking at a car without a stereo, don't be put off, it's a great bargaining tool, and extremely easy to install yourself by visiting your local car supply shop. Technological advances have massively improved car security over the past few years, and having a decent car alarm will lower your insurance premium.

7. **Colour.** Yes, seriously. According to a study by the AA, blue is the most popular choice of car colour. Brown was the least popular choice, followed by gold and yellow. What you may think is a simple aesthetic choice could actually be a major factor in bargaining with a seller, and when you come to sell it on. Overall, twenty-two per cent of people want a silver car and twenty-five per cent have one. Because we Brits are conservative about colour, the manufacturers are, too. Blue, black, grey and silver are a safe bet for them. This means that silver cars have a higher chance of resale than a green car, which is something to take into consideration on the forecourts. White cars aren't usually the first choice of colour. But since the popularity of TV shows like *Geordie Shore* and *The Only Way is Essex*, the white car has soared in popularity. Don't forget, though, that what's cool now might not be in five or more years' time when you're keen to sell your car.

8. **Check-ups.** You wouldn't buy a house without conducting a survey, so the same should go for your motor, preventing unexpected maintenance costs

later. Check the warranty: it depends on your car manufacturer if the warranty extends to the second owner, so it's important to keep this in mind when buying a car brand new.

9. **Background.** Perform a history check on the car to see how many owners it has had, and whether there are any outstanding finance claims. You can enlist the RAC or AA to perform an inspection for as little as £150 for non-members. It's well worth it in the long run to save on unforeseen maintenance costs. Trust your instinct, too: generally in these situations if it seems too good to be true, it probably is.

10. **Trends.** With the cost of petrol rocketing, high fuel consumption cars are depreciating at a higher rate. You may think you're getting a bargain, but it will be at the expense of a larger fuel bill. Always check the m.p.g. (miles per gallon) of your car, as this is one of the most important aspects to owning a vehicle.

'My money-saving tip is something I've come across by accident and was just talking to my local garage owner about – it's really useful to have a car that's the same colour as gaffer tape. Makes repairs a lot cheaper!' – ELINOR, BANGOR

Festivals and special occasions

You know that old ad, a dog is not just for Christmas? Nor is a budget. You're not Santa. Don't pore over an epic Christmas 'to buy' list for everyone in your life and then work out how to pay for it. Calculate how much you can afford to spend first, and then write up your list to suit it. Same with the Christmas dinner. You wouldn't normally buy enough food for forty when you're expecting eight for dinner, so why do so on 25 December? But enough of the Scrooge act: it's still possible to have an amazing Christmas without spending a month's salary. The same is true of big birthdays, weddings and other celebrations. Here's how.

Food

Visit the site lovefoodhatewaste.com: it has brilliant advice about how to avoid buying and cooking too much food for big meals like Christmas dinner – including exact quantities, because who hasn't been left with four tonnes of red cabbage and forty sacks of Brussels sprouts on Boxing Day? There are also thousands of recipes to use up all of your leftovers – just enter the food you've got to use up, and it lists some imaginative meal ideas. Start looking for food deals a couple of months before your celebration. For Christmas, for example, start keeping an eye out for the bargainous food offers in September using hotukdeals. com. Supermarkets often fall over themselves to offer a couple of stand-out offers, like that tin of Quality Street for tuppence or the cheapest turkey this side of Ankara, and this site helps you capitalise on those deals without being sucked into buying too much of the other stuff.

If you're hosting a big meal, don't feel that you have to buy the most expensive brands – let decanting become your best friend. Those fake After Eights you can buy from Aldi? Lay them out prettily on a platter and no one will ever know. That value-range mint sauce? Pour it into a bowl and grin elusively when people ask you for the recipe 'cos it's amazing'. Buying veg? Don't go for the pre-prepared ones, which are far more expensive than chopping and peeling your own. Then get someone else to do it – just be ready with the smilingly-given excuse that you're doing everything else.

When it comes to stocking up on booze, rather than offering guests a huge choice of pricey tipples, either buy a bottle or more of red or white on offer (see page 139 to find the best deals) or make up some cocktails yourself. Sangria is easy, as is mulled wine: just heat one bottle of red wine with 60 grams of brown sugar, a cinnamon stick or sprinkling of ground cinnamon, a dash of nutmeg and dried bayleaf, and a quartered orange. Heat it slowly whilst stirring until the sugar has dissolved, then taste and add more sugar if you want it to be sweeter. Strain whilst serving. Simple, and no one knows the vintage heritage of your red wine, and if you keep topping 'em up they will soon be too drunk to ask.

Presents

Write a list and co-ordinate it with your birthday/Christmas/
etc. budget. That way you can work out that spending £25
on cousin Hetty's foot spa means you'll have less to put
towards cousin Berty's Aston Villa scarf. There's no need to
wait till the last minute to start planning – if you find some
great gifts in the sales, buy them well ahead of time. Just
remember that you did so, and in which high cupboard you
put them. I speak from experience here: finding a haul of
Christmas gifts that you bought in the summer sales in the
middle of February is kick-yourself annoying! Luckily, mine
lasted another year.

Help yourself avoid overspending by using the online
present budget planner at debtadvicefoundation.org/debt-
tools/present-planner. Just tap in your gift requirements
and the site will tell you how your budget is going, where
you've overspent, and who is going to have to have a
cheaper present to make up for it.

Home-made

One of the nicest ways to cut the cost of gift-giving is to
think home-made. This doesn't have to mean jamming a
dodgy old photo into a £1 Ikea photo frame and becoming
known as 'the cheapskate' – you can make amazing
presents, cheaply, that will be far more appreciated by Hetty
and Berty than another foot spa and scarf (didn't you buy
them that last year anyway?). Make up a batch of yummy
hampers, filled with family and friends' favourite foods,

including baked shortbread, gingerbread men or chutneys, and wrap them in crisp cellophane with a twirled ribbon on the top. If you bake and cook in bulk, the time-per-present won't work out too long.

Or make one of those overpriced gift sets that the shops start selling in September yourself. Hot chocolate gift set? Just buy a mug, fill it up with some sachets of instant hot chocolate (if you're feeling really cheap, you could nab them next time you're in a hotel room) plus some bars of posh chocolate and a pack of marshmallows. Again, wrap it all in cellophane and ribbon and it could be mistaken for John Lewis's finest. Cheese and wine gift set? Get out the wrapping materials again, buy a small wooden cheese board (Wilkinson or Ikea sell them for a few pounds), load it up with two or three nice cheeses, plus a bottle of wine or port, and add some crackers.

More ideas: buy a blank notebook, cover it in fabric – much easier to fasten with a strong glue than by sewing – and decorate with a few buttons or a title page. Ta da! You've thoughtfully made someone a scrapbook or journal for their upcoming wedding/university life/new job/travels/baby/etc. Or fill the book with photos – printed off for free using a freebie coupon and an online photo-printing website.

For another big source of home-made presents, learn to knit – or try to remember how you used to do it, ooh, a few decades ago. Then buy some decent wool in bulk and knit scarves for friends and family alike. Once you have learnt the basic steps of casting on, knitting a row, and casting off (easy instructions in words and diagrams here: learn2knit. co.uk and there are videos on YouTube), it's easy to knit in front of the TV, whilst on the train, or mid phone call, and you'll quickly be bestowing knitted gifts on everyone you know. Learn how to do knitting and practically every craft that exists at craftsy.com – online courses that you do have to pay for, but are comprehensive and cheaper than 'real world' courses.

Vouchers

Another way to personalise gifts the recipients will really like is to prepare home-made gift vouchers. Does your partner absolutely love your chocolate fudge biscuits but you can rarely be bothered to make them? Give him a cookie jar full of them, plus a voucher promising to refill it whenever you're presented with it. My cousin did that four years ago, and the deal was so popular his wife has asked for the same gift year after year. But if you're worried about spending every evening for the rest of your life refilling the cookie jar, just add some carefully worded terms and conditions at the bottom like all the 'real' vouchers have . . .

Other voucher ideas could include giving your time – perhaps free babysitting to your overtired new-parent friends, or taking their kids on a day trip to a cinema or museum, or offering to rustle up a three-course meal. Make the coupons look more pro by making a free voucher using the software at giftcertificatefactory.com.

For another kind of subscription, magazine deals can also be picked up for a song – a lot of the big glossy mags offer cheap deals that can make a £5-a-month magazine cost as little as £1. Recipients will never know about the cost reduction, but will love receiving their present in regular doses throughout the year. Many subscriptions also come with free gifts, like make-up sets or toiletries, which you could use yourself, give as an extra to your recipient, or save up as a present for someone else. The website magazinesubscriptions.co.uk lists streams of deals from various providers.

Be wary of buying store vouchers at the moment though; the turmoil on the high street has seen a string of retailers including Habitat, Barratts, PriceLess Shoes, Jane Norman and Focus DIY collapse into administration over the past year. If you buy a voucher for a retailer that shuts down, it's unlikely to be usable. If you do want to buy someone gift vouchers, opt for a wider scheme instead, like one covering a whole shopping centre or the One4all gift card from the Post Office, which can buy goods from 17,000 UK outlets, including toy store Hamleys, plus Argos, Boots, B&Q, Debenhams, and Pizza Express.

'Fill your car up with petrol when it's cold, say early in the morning or late at night, because you'll get more fuel for the same price – petrol expands in the heat.' –
RAPHAEL, HUDDERSFIELD

If you've got kids, put them to good present-making use. Grandparents will love a personalised present from the children (and you) – as long as they can see some effort has gone into it. Craft superstores like Hobbycraft have cheap canvasses with which, depending on the children's ages, they could paint a family portrait, or record their footprint and frame it. Teenagers could make compilation CDs of your old favourites for your friends. Kids can help with the décor too. At Christmas, for example, instead of buying yet another poinsettia that will make it to the table centrepiece then die shortly after, make snowflake paper chains or spray pine cones with artificial snow. Decorate pound-shop baubles with paint or glitter.

When your creativity has been exhausted and you're back to traditional present-buying, remember all the usual laws of money-saving shopping, spending and saving both online and on the high street (see pages 13–27). Source bargain-bucket stocking fillers from charity stores and pound shops, or pick up a pile of cheap paperbacks from a second-hand bookshop. For more unusual gifts, etsy.com links up creative people around the world making a cornucopia of goodies like handmade puppets, vintage items, knitted scarfs and more, and because most of the sellers don't have the overheads of a shop, there are some bargain goodies. Others can be found on notonthehighstreet.com – usually not cheap, but beautiful and personalised.

All these ideas are just as useful for birthdays and other special occasions as they are for Christmas. And remember to stock up a present cupboard throughout the year – see page 110–11.

Cards

I'm not particularly artistic – ask me to draw a pig and you'll still end up having to guess what it is – but one creative thing that I can do is make greetings cards. You don't have to be Tracey Emin to easily whip up a stack of the type of homemade cards that shops charge £4 for – you just need some good materials, and these are easy to accumulate on the cheap. I always work in bulk – you can still do personalised cards this way, just sit down and think about whose birthdays are coming up, and do them all in one go to save time.

Every year or so I buy a stack of plain ivory folded pieces of card from a cheap stationery shop – I usually visit The Works (theworks.co.uk) but Hobbycraft or a local haberdashery will also fit the bill – for a couple of quid. Then whenever I am sent a particularly colourful brochure in the post, or other decorative greetings cards with little paper flowers or other details on, or see any free fabric samples, buttons or ribbons, I put them in my craft kit (aka a cardboard box in the corner of my living room).

To make a card, I usually glue a square of fabric in the middle, stick a square of card in a different colour on top, then add a personalised touch such as a wired rose from a shop-bought birthday cake long ago, or a dried flower, posh sticker, or little photo stuck on to corrugated cardboard to make it look 3D. Sometimes I'll make something personal to the recipient, other times it's more generic. If it's for a birthday, I usually add another thing I've picked up from the craft shop: a silver sticker off a pack of 500 reading 'Happy birthday' that's available for £1. Using these – rather than my own wonkily written 'happy birtday' with an 'h' belatedly squeezed in – make the cards look premium. An evening spent doing this will produce between ten and twenty cards, lasting a couple of months, and is fun as well as economical.

Planning ahead on cards will avoid wasting loads of

dosh. Posting birthday cards in advance will avoid the need for first-class stamps, whilst for Christmas, find out when the Post Office's last posting date is for sending cards and parcels both in the UK and, if relevant, abroad and post them before then. Look at the last posting dates for free or cheap delivery for online retailers, too – and if you're sending gifts to friends or family who live far away, get the e-tailer to send them direct to avoid shelling out twice. As for wrapping paper – is there a bigger waste of money out there? If you're very keen to use it, see if you can wangle free gift-wrapping when buying on the high street. If not, reuse one of those gift bags you received at some point earlier in the year (just cut off the 'Dear Fred, Love Pootsie' label) or wrap gifts in a few layers of newspaper and smarten them up with some ribbon. A huge reel of ribbon costs £2 at a place like Hobbycraft or you might find one for half that at a pound store.

Most importantly, never let present-giving push you into scary levels of debt. If times are really tough, talk to family and friends about not buying presents for everyone, and making them either just for the kids, or setting up a Secret Santa/Birthday Bunny scheme where everyone buys one gift or everyone puts a smaller amount of money towards a big day out. Or consider setting an upper limit on gifts so no one feels embarrassed about what they have spent.

Weddings

What's the quickest way for a bride to shed pounds before a wedding? Use the 'w' word when talking to suppliers. OK, it's not the best dieting tip. Or joke. But the Big Day industry has become one enormous money-spinner, and using the 'wedding' word before visiting a florist, caterer, venue or other supplier will send your bill soaring. I know – I'm currently planning my own.

So what's the solution? Well, the average wedding in Britain costs more than £20,000. You could buy a house for that in some parts of the country – or a village of houses in some other countries. Anyway, since you might soon want to buy your own house, or maybe are currently paying off a mortgage on an existing one, it's a useful reminder of the importance of wedding/marriage prioritisation.

Starting your lives together in debt because of a big white day isn't a recipe for happiness. In fact, the very opposite: financial worries are often cited as a major reason for divorce. So the first rule of your nuptials should be this: don't overspend on your big day if doing so means starting life in debt, or deeper in the red than you otherwise would be. It's really, really not worth it. And to that end, the second rule for wedding-planning bliss should be this: don't pore over celebrity or enormously over-the-top weddings in bridal magazines – it'll only make you want things you don't need or can't afford. That's the reason I started wedding-planning whilst dreaming of a photo booth and vintage ice-cream van on site on our big day. Once I realised either would cost something like £1,000, I realised the necessity of always reminding myself that neither a Mr Whippy-mobile nor a ton of passport pictures would be crucial recipes for a big celebration, and nor would they boost our chances of a happy marriage. And you can easily set up a camera on a tripod in front of a white sheet, with a box of fancy dress gear nearby, to make your own DIY photobooth, if you feel the need.

I've spent umpteen weekends over the past few years celebrating at weddings of my friends and family – and I've developed an extra-special interest in them over the past . . . oooh, six months three weeks and two days that I've been engaged. I now know that a local wedding in an imaginatively decorated hall with gorgeous bunting, jam jars holding posies, friends and family responsible for various parts of the food, an iPod with the couple's favourite songs acting as a DJ, plus a disposable-camera-led scavenger hunt for the kids really can be just as lovely as a lavish celebration for hundreds of people that the couple don't really know. It's all about the feeling your friends and family create, not about a twenty-course banquet that you and your fiancé (or family or friends) have struggled to afford and are left feeling stressed about paying for.

The first step to wedding planning should be setting a budget. This might involve some awkward conversations with parents or other relatives, but it's so much better to get them out the way first than to spend endless weekends visiting dream castle venues or falling in love with Elton John's favourite photographer, only to later discover that booking either would swallow up your entire wedding fund fourteen times over.

Instead, sit down with your partner and/or family and work out who is paying for what, or is willing to offer a contribution to your wedding. There are lots of free online wedding budgets to help: check out Google weddings, visit the blog whimsicalwonderlandweddings.com or check out hitched.co.uk, all of which have an excellent range of free tools. Beyond the budget-makers, they also host seating-plan software, guest list help, music playlist tools and menu-makers.

'Use Freecycle. I'm a big fan. I've used it for years to list anything I no longer use, and have used it to find things I've needed, too. Over the years, I have got the following items for free: garden shed, trampoline, car seats for children, plants and guinea pigs.' – KYLIE, CAMBRIDGESHIRE

Once you know your budget, you'll need to work out exactly what you want to spend it on, so try to jot down everything that you are thinking of booking for the big day: from dress and dance floor to ceremony transport, from a hotel room in which to spend your first married night together, to photographer and hairdresser. Next, work out your top priorities. If you're a huge fan of arty photos, you'll want a professional photographer. If your fiancé is a music buff, a band might be a must. If you're a lass who's a fan of the natural look, you might forgo a hairdresser and make-up artist and spend the savings on a dessert buffet or embossed gold-leaf invitations – whatever your most important ideas are, get them to the top of the list. Once that work is done, the next step is to shop around to work out the rough costs of what you want – the venue(s) and catering will probably cost more than half of your total – and see what you can afford.

Because if you've always wanted to get married in a particular venue and it costs two-thirds of your budget, then work out what else you'd have to cut back on (maybe asking friends to be snappers at different points during the day, or finding a colleague who's a dab hand with blending to do the bride's make-up, or buying a second-hand wedding dress) and whether that's acceptable or you'd prefer to find another venue.

What you shouldn't – ever – do, is raise your budget to fit your wish list. Yes, the dreamy wedding magazines make it tough to keep a grip on reality, but remind yourself of that cold, hard fact about the correlation between debt and divorce, and remember what's important. Now, on to a ton of money-saving nuptial ideas, so you can have the big day you've dreamed of without blowing the budget.

The venue

Consider a package. All the big hotel chains, plus a growing number of independent hotels, now offer all-inclusive wedding deals. Both Holiday Inn and Britannia Hotels have recently offered £999 and £1,500 wedding deals, for example, which include a Bucks Fizz reception and wedding breakfast for between thirty and fifty guests, decorative touches like balloons and flower centrepieces on the tables, followed by an evening reception buffet for eighty to a hundred guests. These all-inclusive deals can be a good way to keep your budget under control.

Don't dismiss any potential venues out of hand. Be imaginative. Hotels and country houses might look the most glamorous to the naked eye, but remember church halls, local barns, fields with a marquee, a friend's garden or a local club can all be transformed with the help of some cool decorations, floral arrangements, balloons and personalised touches like photos of you and your fiancé(e) artfully dotted around the room.

Don't only consider a Saturday. Weekend dates are always the most popular for weddings, but a midweek option can trigger big discounts on venues, caterers, bands, photographers and even suit hire firms and hairdressers. Oh, and whilst your nearest and dearest will obviously take the day off work to celebrate with you, those distant cousins who you wouldn't mind cutting off the list anyway might not feel the same . . . meaning they turn down your invite and give you the opportunity to invite a friend you'd much prefer to be there, or just save a bit of money!

Think laterally. Wedding ceremonies can take place in a huge array of places. Churches, synagogues and other religious sites tend to charge upwards of £200. Extras like choirs, musicians and bell-ringers will all add a few hundred pounds to your bill. Registry offices are cheaper, usually £100 if you've just a few guests, although the cost will rise if you need a larger venue.

Remember, having your ceremony and party in the same place could save on extra costs like wedding cars and/or guest transport. But if you do split your day, it's worth seeing if you can club together with another couple marrying on the same day. If your ceremony venue, for example, is hosting a wedding either before or after your celebrations, then ask the venue owner or organiser if the other bridal party would be interested in going halves on the cost of flowers and decorations. Then just hope you have similar taste . . .

The dress

Start by visiting a couple of bridal shops to decide what kind of dress you want. If nothing else, it can be a lovely experience, with free champers in some West End stores. But designer meringues can easily cost thousands, or even tens of thousands of pounds, and there are a gaggle of ways to cut back. If you've fallen in love with a particular dress, check out stillwhite.co.uk, where designer dresses from big names such as Suzanne Neville, Caroline Castigliano and Pronovias are on sale in a huge range of prices and sizes. Other good sites listing second-hand (but let's be clear here, unlike usual vintage wares this really just means once worn and then dry-cleaned – as close to new as you'll find) include preloved.co.uk and sellmyweddingdress. co.uk. For made-to-measure designs, local dressmakers will often offer good deals – but make sure you've seen their past work and are happy with it. Department stores like Debenhams and House of Fraser, plus discount store TK Maxx also offer off-the-peg dresses that usually cost around £500, but brides-to-be report snapping them up for a steal in the sales.

Consider China. Sounds weird, but China's wedding dress industry is booming, and you can pick up a bargainous made-in-China wedding dress via eBay – just search for 'made-to-measure wedding dress'. You'll need to do your research, though; ensure the seller has a top rating, and ask lots of questions about sizing, delivery and design. Request fabric samples, check reviews and get in contact with past brides to ask how they found the experience with particular sellers/tailors. Remember to factor in extras in to the cost: you'll have to pay for postage (which can be as much as £75) plus VAT and customs duty of around thirty per cent of the agreed fee.

Other sources of inexpensive wedding dresses include Oxfam, which has eleven specialist bridal shops and lists its dresses online at tinyurl.com/oxfamweddingdress. Some of the dresses are even brand-new donations by designers. And keep an eye out for sample sales too – they're listed on the events page of bridal magazines, and free online at sites like bridesmagazine.co.uk. Or ask if there are any antique bridal gowns being kept in the family – a bride in her mother or grandmother's wedding dress (which can easily be tweaked by an alteration expert) often triggers family members' amazing memories of an earlier big day and can become a family tradition.

The bride

You can save a few hundred pounds (not that kind – the gyms section comes later) by forgoing a professional make-up artist and hairdresser. Since both usually insist on trials before the wedding day, they can easily cost more than £200 each. But instead, you could book an early morning visit at a department store's beauty counter, like MAC or Clinique, where the beauticians will do your make-up for you for free, or show you how to do it yourself. You might want to buy the lippie or concealer for touch-ups. Or ask if a local college runs reduced pampering deals: they will often provide hairdressing students who will do up-dos for just a few pounds (you can have a trial first to make sure you're happy). Or enlist a talented friend. But remember to practise first to avoid panic on the day.

Numbers

When the number of attendees balloons, so does the cost. So try to cut out guests – it's best to explain to anyone who might get upset that you're really stuck on numbers due to the venue's capacity or costs, rather than let them find out by seeing the photos on Facebook and getting upset. Or consider inviting a few close members of your family and friends to the ceremony and meal, and the rest for a boogie sesh later on. If family members are demanding you include distant relatives or old family friends, gently but firmly explain it's not financially feasible. But be aware that if they then offer a financial contribution, it could make it difficult to turn down Great Aunt Sybil after all – so don't use this as an excuse to exclude Syb and co. from your big day.

The extras

Be frank with suppliers like florists and photographers: tell them your budget, and ask what they can supply for that. Many are offering recession-era deals, with photographers, for example, offering quotes for just their time plus a high-res CD of all the shots. That way, you can receive hundreds of brilliant pictures, but cut out the cost of the (very expensive) albums. You can easily make your own on one of the amazing photobook websites out there; my favourite for professional-looking albums and books is blurb.com, but the likes of snapfish.com and photobox.com are cheaper and more straightforward.

Seek out several quotes from suppliers, and then bargain with them. Times aren't just tough for you and me – they will have experienced a decline in business and most will be willing to chuck in an extra album or more if you ask. We're paying the full package price for my photographer, but getting albums for all the family included, plus prints and a CD of the pictures, so there won't be any extra costs.

Try to go local: when we found out we needed a power generator for our wedding party, I was getting miserable receiving £2,000 quotations from national firms until my mum contacted a local company who came up with a much-reduced offer.

Think of your friends. No, not how lovely they are, but how useful they are! If one is an ace baker, ask them if they'll make you a wedding cake or piled-up cupcakes as your wedding present. They will often enjoy being included in the big day as well as doing you a favour. Any

DJs, florists, printers, or confident-types who could MC in your family? Know someone with a posh car, or holiday home for a honeymoon? All you can do is ask . . .

Invites

There are hundreds of free invite-design sites on the web – check out weddingchicks.com, smilebox.com or vistaprint. co.uk for self-designed cards. Or work up your own design and take it to a local printer – much cheaper than an invitation specialist.

For something different that will surprise people, check out paperlesspost.com. I used this site, and although the cards are online only, the designs are so brilliant that they are really memorable: an image of an envelope with your friend's name 'handwritten' on the front lands in their inbox, then, when they click to open it, the invite slides out of the envelope and unfolds like a paper one in front of their eyes. You can secure ten invites on the site for free, then the rest are paid for, but every time you recommend a friend it triggers another ten free credits. So I just posted my 'recommend a friend' link on Twitter and soon secured enough invites to send to all my friends and family for free.

Decorations

There are so many free or cheap options with decorations. Paper chains, candles, bunting cut out of lovely vintage fabric (check out curtain superstores to source free samples and offcuts), beach shells to hold place names. The vintage look is very now, and luckily it's easy to reproduce spectacular results for little money. Old jam jars, for example, can be washed out, then filled with wild flowers; paper doilies are super cheap but look brilliant en masse on tables, mismatched old crockery from charity shops can help transform a boring table setting into an eye-catching one. Double up decorations with favours: you can buy twenty plant pots for £1 from pound-shops, then fill them with soil and a lavender or rosemary plant cutting, make labels with guests' names on, and you've got a thoughtful, home-made favour that doubles up as a place card and will fill the air with a gorgeous scent.

Eating and drinking

Food and wine are usually the biggest cost, after the venue. So think about whether you really need or want a three-course meal: barbecues, roasts and buffets, for example, can be just as nice. Ask favourite neighbourhood cafés if they do external catering – they're often much cheaper than stand-alone caterers – and you can rent glasses for free from supermarkets including Waitrose. If you haven't found a friend to make your cake, consider DIY – a simple sponge is easy, and you can buy blocks of ready-to-roll-icing to make it look pro. Or make cupcakes and layer them on a tiered cake stand.

Boring but crucial

Don't forget wedding insurance. It might seem like an annoying expense, but if the worst should happen and your caterer, venue or florist should go bust, an insurance policy may be the difference between your day going ahead and not. Compare the price at moneysupermarket.com/wedding-insurance; cover will cost between £15 and £500, depending on the scale of your do. The aspects to include are supplier failure, cancellation and accidents.

Honeymoon

Here you'll need to stick to all the tips in the holiday chapter (see below) to secure the best deal for your break. But some extra honeymoon-specific tips to cut the cost include setting up a honeymoon list for your guests to contribute to instead of gifts, asking friends or family with holiday homes if they might be willing to let you stay for a bit, and milking every single opportunity to tell the world you're on honeymoon! It can often lead to upgrades on flights, hotel rooms and even free drinks during restaurant meals. Remember to take your wedding certificate with you as proof – apparently there are a lot of fake just-marrieds going around trying to steal the real McCoy's thunder.

Holidays

Ah, holidays. Like everyone else, I absolutely love them. But nowadays, with a job to tackle, wedding to plan, book to write, flat to maintain, etc. etc., I just don't have the time that I used to spend researching, price-checking, re-price-checking, re-re-re-price-checking, discovering all that price-checking has pushed up the initial price, finding a replacement hotel/flight/etc. – and eventually, slowly, getting round to booking.

But luckily, with a few tools in mind, booking the best-value break doesn't need to take long at all. First, though, just before you start dreaming of warm beach sand between your toes, the adrenalin of a tricky manoeuvre on the slopes or adventurous fun elsewhere, pause to think about that term 'good value'. Sometimes you'll want to splurge on a more luxurious break, other times it might be just a cheap and cheerful escape you're looking for. Work out what you want, then use the tips below to pay the lowest possible price to secure that trip you're dreaming of – leaving a wad of extra cash to splurge on cocktails, excursions or culture when you're there.

Accommodation

Holiday accommodation doesn't have to mean a hotel. You could check in to someone's home and pay very little, or even swap your own base with someone else's for free. You could check out one of the new brand of upmarket hostels that are more like boutique hotels. Or maybe you'd prefer the bunk bed and dorm of the hostel of old – there are still plenty around, too! Meanwhile, camping has morphed into glamping for those looking for a little more luxury, and demand for camper-van breaks is booming. Renting a holiday home – especially if you do so with another family or friends – can also be a really cheap source of accommodation. If you're still not impressed and want to stick to a hotel, read up on the new ways to guarantee you can sit by the pool knowing your room rate is the lowest out of all the lounger-lazers surrounding you. Here's how:

Hotels

Gone are the days when you'd call up Moira at your local travel agency and she'd guarantee you the room you had last year for the same six nights of this summer, at a pretty similar price, too. Nowadays, we all want to travel more, stay in better hotels, and pay less for the privilege. Luckily, the internet has made the seemingly impossible a lot easier. First, you have to work out where, geographically, you want to stay, and which hotels would be best for doing so. Obviously, for a city or beach hotel, one that's in the centre of town or close to the waves will inevitably work out more expensive than one that requires a bus ride to the shops or shore. Maybe you'd prefer to pay less for a luxury hotel out of the way but with a better swimming pool, spa, etc., or maybe you just want a base that's bang in the middle of the city's culture, beach, shopping, etc., but has more basic amenities. Just work out your priorities and find a few hotels that fit the bill. Once that's done, it's time to get them for the cheapest possible price.

Your first stop should be a price-comparison website. My favourite way to do this is to tap in the name of one of my hotel possibilities on tripadvisor.com, and then type in the dates of the trip. Then click the tick boxes next to the various deal-scanning sites, and select 'search'. The site will automatically activate pop-up boxes showing the prices you can get those rooms for, on those nights, if you book via expedia.co.uk, hotels.com, booking.com, thomascook.com, otel.com or venere.com. You can also read the usual reviews of the hotel to help you work out if you want to stay there. If you're put off that one, or struggling to put together a shortlist, use these comparison sites to find a list of hotels available in your desired destination which you can then narrow down with the help of star ratings, amenities, location, and so on. Other hotel comparison sites worth a visit include trivago.co.uk and travelsupermarket.com. But make sure you're comparing like-for-like on all these deals, as some rooms may include taxes and/or breakfast whilst other rates may add costs on at the point of booking.

So you've secured an array of prices. But there are two more steps before booking. First, to be absolutely certain that you're getting the very best deal around, it's worth contacting the hotel direct. Sure, check their website too, but this is one area in which web doesn't always win. Often hotel sites advertise extortionate rates, so phone up (if it's an international call use the cost-cutting tips on page 244) and simply, but politely, ask their best rate, and then ask if they will beat the quote you have found online. Sometimes they will do so; if not, see if they will consider throwing in extras such as free breakfasts or airport transfers that could lower the overall cost of your break. Note also that when you book direct it's likely to be more flexible, with a friendlier cancellation policy, than booking via an agent – but check, as this will differ, depending on the hotel.

And if you do decide to book online, remember to secure cashback. (See page 19 to find out how to do so – and remember to clear your cookies or use another computer if you've spent time on the site already, to avoid invalidating your claim.)

Or, if you've not found a stellar deal or hotel that you fancy, one last idea is to consider going for a secret one. Because big hotels – particularly the chains – don't like to advertise their emptiness, they have started shifting any unfilled rooms via brokers like hotwire.com or lastminute. com. The former just does 'secret' hotels, whilst the latter has a special section devoted to them. You will be told the hotel's location, amenities and star rating, but not its name, until you've paid the (non-refundable) cost.

On the face of it, that's all hunky-dory, but in reality, one four-star hotel will often be vastly superior to another, so you'll want to know more about it to work out if you've got a decent deal. Luckily, with a bit of online sleuthing, that's pretty easy. Sometimes, a simple Google search of the hotel's description (copy a key sentence direct from the secret hotel's description and put it in quotation marks for an exact search) will bring up its listing on another website, revealing its identity. At other times, you'll have to be just a little more savvy, and rely on the experiences of holidaymakers who have previously secured secret hotel rooms and revealed them online. Enter your potential hotel's details at secrethotelsrevealed.co.uk to see if it's there. If not, the webheads at tinyurl.com/forum-hotels have identified many more. Once you've worked out which hotel you're looking at, you can carry out the above steps to find out its cheapest advertised rate and work out if the secret deal is actually a good one. Remember, though, it's not guaranteed that your detective work will be accurate – so you'll still have to cope with a bit of an excited/anxious feeling on the 'buy' screen as you wait to find out what you've paid for.

Do remember, too, that new rules mean that anyone who buys at least two components of a holiday – hotel, flight, etc. – from the same provider is now covered by the money-back scheme run by ABTA (see below). If buying separately, and you are spending over £100, try to pay by credit card – at least for the deposit – to secure your cash (see credit card section, page 227).

Hostels

Wait, wait, wait. Don't skip on to the next section without at least considering them. Hostels are no longer just for Kevin and Perry-type teenagers: many have family rooms, many more are filled with 'silver surfers', and lots are now very upmarket.

As a teenager, when I toured Europe with friends, we travelled by coach and slept on metal bunk beds at hostels where – at one particularly desperate stop – we had to buy sheets because the only available berths came with worryingly yellow-stained bedding. Maybe you had the same experience. But hostels really have changed. I stayed in one in Berlin that had more in common with a luxe boutique hotel than some of Europe's so-called hotels, which are so ropey you can only deduce the owners stuck their own stars on the door after cutting them out of silver foil.

Cool hostels have retained the communal areas and big breakfast tables that always made them far more social than sterile hotel bars and lounges, but a large number also offer en-suite rooms. And white, pristine bed sheets. There's often a lot more individuality and local touches than in international chain hotels, with rooms decorated by local artists and full of interior design touches.

In Paris for example, a hostel called Oops! is bang in the centre of town, with colour-blocked, design-led rooms – breakfast and Wi-Fi included – located near several metro stations (Place d'Italie and Les Gobelins) plus a Vélib' station for cheap cycling on the city-wide bike scheme. It's air conditioned, all rooms are en-suite, and rates begin at €23 a night (see oops-paris.com). Or check out Plas Curig (snowdoniahostel.co.uk), a new, boutique hostel in the middle of Snowdonia national park with John Lewis-style bunk bed rooms with Welsh wool blankets, rustic design, plus a well-stocked library, dining room and kitchen, bike storage and lounge. A dorm room costs from £22.50, or a double/twin room is £25 per person.

Further afield, I hear great things about Kadir's Tree Houses in Olympus, Turkey, a complex of a hundred tree houses, fifteen cabins and ten dorm rooms, plus camping facilities from £9 a night (see kadirstreehouses.com). It's not one for those seeking peace and quiet – several bars are also strung around the trees – and the accommodation is more basic than elsewhere, but a night in a tree house is definitely one to shout about on Facebook.

Find more cool, chic or crazy options at hostelbooks.com,

which lists 3,500 hostels around the world and offers a price guarantee where it will double the difference if a cheaper rate is found elsewhere. Or check out hostelworld.com, which has far more choice – about 27,000 properties in 180 countries – but does charge a booking fee.

Holiday homes

Renting out a holiday home or apartment has always been a popular way to save money on accommodation abroad. But since the start of the credit crunch, more families have starting renting out their properties, making bargains easier to come by. Obviously, it'll be a different kind of holiday to one based in a hotel. You'll have to buy your own cornflakes or croissants, rather than enjoy that pile of waffles or perfect sunny-side up egg at the hotel breakfast buffet spread. You'll have to clean the place yourself, unless you pay extra for a cleaner, and you may have fewer facilities on-site, unless your rental home is on a resort.

But there are major bonuses too: more privacy, and no nosy Norberts banging around noisily in the room next door at 6 a.m. (unless you travelled with Norbert, in which case it's your fault anyway). Come and go when you please, guarantee you'll like the food on offer (because you'll be making it – although more expensive lets will often offer chef rental for extra fees), and feel more relaxed about your kids' safety if you opt for a child-friendly pad. It's also a fab opportunity to go away with friends and, since renting a six-bedroom property will never be six times more expensive than a one-bed, larger groups mean better opportunities to save money too.

How to do it? Holiday homes are advertised everywhere from local papers and newsagents' windows to the internet. The latter is obviously the most convenient place to start your search. Big aggregator sites like holidaylettings.co.uk (more than 50,000 holiday homes in 116 countries), holiday-rentals.co.uk (300,000 self-catering cottages, apartments and villas) and ownersdirect.co.uk (33,000) all have a huge range of options. The websites allow you to hunt by location (country, area, resort or suburb); dates (to look for properties available when you are); group size; included features (pool, wheelchair access, pet friendly etc.); and budget. It's a good idea to make a list of properties you like the look of, then contact the owners and find out about availability. Be aware that you may not have the same rights as when booking other kinds of accommodation. The guarantee of the Association of British Travel Agents (ABTA) only covers travel agents and tour operators, so if renting direct from an owner, be sure to check the terms and conditions of your travel insurance (or buy a specialist holiday lettings policy). You'll want it to cover your deposit and any later payments against potential problems like fraud, the villa not existing, or late cancellation by the owners.

Other ways to protect yourself include researching the holiday home in depth. How long has it been advertised? What reviews have other renters provided, either on agency sites or tripadvisor.co.uk? Look it up on the street view function of Google Maps (maps.google.com) to check the reality of the villa or apartment matches the online pictures. Contact the owners via the phone to quiz them on normal issues like the logistics of getting to the villa, but use the chat to work out if you find them trustworthy, and ask for their home address and phone number as an emergency contact during your stay. Never send a deposit without receiving and checking through a written contract, and if possible pay via a credit card or a credit card linked to online payment provider PayPal to boost your protection. (see page 227 on credit cards). Oh, and once you're there, snap pictures of the place on arrival. Not just of the beeeeeautiful view so you can immediately show off to friends at home on Facebook, but of any damage so you can prove you didn't do it. It's best to do so whilst the property's owner or manager – whoever lets you in – is still on site.

'One good way I've found that saves money is to holiday in Britain – but not in London. Alternative cities with plenty of attractions and their own individual charm include Manchester, Edinburgh and Bristol. Also smaller places such as Harrogate, Padstow and Bath are historical and picturesque . . . Who needs to go abroad?' – JOSH, WORCESTERSHIRE

Package breaks

They might have fallen out of fashion, but don't forget the old humble package holiday. There's no need for it to turn into *Coach Trip* – nowadays they're just a cheap way to organise an all-in-one flight, airport transfer and hotel deal. The downside is the loss of flexibility – package trips are created to attract the majority of people, and will only fit your bill if you're willing to go to a fairly traditional destination, for one or two weeks or ten days.

The very cheapest time to buy a package deal is very close to departure date. The tour operators have already booked their plane and reserved accommodation, and if the seats and rooms are empty, they start to panic. So they cut prices, and you swoop in. Outside of school holiday times will trigger the biggest bargains. Use sites like travelsupermarket.com, travelzoo.co.uk and teletextholidays.co.uk to find a trip that takes your fancy. The more flexible you can be with dates and destinations, the more likely you are to find a great deal. (Although sometimes the offers are good enough that it's cheaper to book a package even if you only want to actually use the flight element.)

Now, once you've tracked down a holiday that tickles your fancy, don't just book it. Don't Thomas Cook it either. Well, not necessarily. Since lots of travel agents sell the same package holidays, it's worth contacting several on the phone (their details will be listed on the above sites) to see if you can wangle a further discount. Make sure any prices you are quoted include booking fees and transfer costs.

The other major benefit of package holidays in the

doldrums of the current economic climate is this: since airlines have been folding all over the place (and I'm not talking about the paper variety), the protection of ATOL (Air Travel Organisers' Licensing) and ABTA could come in handy. They provide protection in the event of the travel company's financial failure, meaning if an airline or hotel etc. collapses, you'll be able to get a refund if you're still at home, or have an alternative route home or accommodation organised on your behalf if you're already away. Check that your package is covered before booking.

House swap

It's the latest big trend in holiday-making. Not only do you save tons of money on accommodation (which you can then spend on your actual holiday) but you live life like a local, not a tourist. House swaps won't be for everyone. If you're a paranoid Monica-from-*Friends* type who would spend your entire holiday breaking out in a sweat because you're worried about your sparklingly clean oven at home, it's probably not for you. And if your home is packed full of delicate museum-worthy pieces, the effort of house-swapping might just be too much.

But otherwise, have a gander at a couple of home swapping houses and see what you could get for free – and you could soon be convinced. A couple of my friends swapped their two-up, two-down semi in a suburb of London for a five-bedroom, brand-new seaside apartment in Tel Aviv. On their return, they said the only bad thing about the swap was the vague guilt they had felt every now and then – 'Wow, the other guys have got a raw deal'.

Often home-swappers will leave you detailed info packs, not just about their pad, but the neighbourhood, giving you access to the local delis and best restaurants that Bob from Bournemouth would never find when relying on *Lonely Planet*. If they're friendly with their neighbours, often they too will help you have a great holiday.

But you'll have to do your research, and work hard on your own home before departure. The biggest home-swap sites include homeforexchange.com, and homelink.org.uk. There are varying membership fees – from £71.40 for a year's membership at Home for Exchange to £115 a year at HomeLink, but they shouldn't be your only consideration. Only sign up with a site that has lots of homes in the region you want to visit, and few in the UK, because it will boost your chances of finding a swap. Consider one of the specialist sites where you'll find swappers who match your interests – the *Guardian* has a site at guardianhomeexchange.co.uk, for example, which costs £35 a year, although it's best for UK-based swaps. For parents, the National Childbirth Trust's ncthouseswap.ning.com is worth a visit, whilst sabbaticalhomes.com matches up academics looking for longer swaps, but is open to all – it also has listings of home rentals and home-sitting services required or desired. At another site, swapmycitypad.com, gold members (£49.99 a year) can join a network of professionals such as lawyers or doctors.

Once you've joined, you'll have to write your place up, and it will feel like you're joining a dating agency. How to make it sound nice, homely, accessible – but realistic? What is the best light to take the photos in? Is it worth mentioning the traffic is kind of noisy, but you don't hear it anymore, or is that best glossed over? Take your time and use others' examples as a starting point. Be upbeat, but always honest – better to secure the right match than disappoint the swapper and mar your reputation with a bad review.

When you're up and listed, it's time to start contacting homeowners in the area you're interested in visiting. It's likely you'll have to contact a fair few before you find someone willing to come to your place and on the dates you have in mind. Once you've found a place you like the look of, do the same sleuth work as for holiday home rentals (see above) – plus a little more. As well as using Google Maps to check out the home and neighbourhood, use Google itself to look up the potential swapper, and perhaps his or her business. It's worth talking on the phone or even via a video link-up like Skype or Apple's Facetime to find out if you trust and like each other. Many swappers draw up a mutual contract detailing arrival and departure dates, what will be included in the swap (cars, local travelcards, airport pick-up arrangements etc.), and always ask for references.

Before your departure date, make sure your home insurance isn't invalidated by a swap, lock away valuables, and make sure you're leaving your home spotlessly clean. Make a little space in your wardrobes, clear the fridge of any past-its-best food and leave a spare set of towels and linen. It's a nice idea to have a few welcoming foods in situ too. It's also a good idea to provide a booklet with info on how to use your home appliances, a local contact for emergencies, and a little insider knowledge on your area, such as any favourite restaurants and shops, plus transport tips. Once you've gone to this effort once, you can reuse the booklet for future swaps.

Couch-surfing

Nothing to do with prancing around on a sofa pretending to be riding the waves, everything to do with a free or very cheap route to holiday accommodation: that's couch-surfing. It's a purely online phenomenon, with one of the biggest sites being couchsurfing.org, which is like a social networking site for travellers. Its two million-plus members include hosts willing to offer a free place to stay and wannabe couch-surfers, all of who have Facebook-style user profiles, photos and friend requests, and eBay-style feedback. It's not just couches that are up for offer – there are plenty of spare bedrooms, or just spare floors. Other popular sites include airbnb.com, wheretosleep.co.uk, swapmycitypad.com and crashpadder.com.

Garden-surfing

For something different, campinmygarden.com offers free or cheap camping in people's gardens around the world. The facilities range from what it calls 'bamping' – basic camping, a patch of grass – to 'glamping', aka glamorous camping, which may include toilets and a cooked breakfast. Most of its bases are currently in the UK, but it's especially good for finding places to stay near major sporting or music events, when hotels would normally be very expensive. Most garden rentals cost from £10 a night. Elsewhere, camping can provide the ultimate low-cost holiday. Outdoor shops like Millets and Blacks sell family camping kits, and the likes of Argos sell a family tent, mats and sleeping bags for well under £100 – and you can use them for endless cheap breaks in Britain and abroad. To find a campsite in the UK, check out find-a-campsite.co.uk and coolcamping.co.uk.

Transport

It's natural to spend a while hunting for the best holiday accommodation. You're going to spend a fair whack of your precious annual leave lounging around in the place, so checking it out – finding your favourite beach loungers and the best-located place for bars, culture, etc. – seems fair game. But hunting down the travelling options to get there? Not so much. Unless you're zooming around via private jet (in which case, can I have a lift?), you probably just want to get from A to B by the cheapest, safest, quickest route possible. Now, you'll have to do your own research with a map to work out what your options are, depending on where you're going. But flight to ferry, here are the cheapest ways to source your journey.

'Don't exchange foreign currency at UK airports. The Post Office or banks will offer far better rates' – TAUQUEER, LONDON

Flights

Upgrades

Sometimes you just want a bit of luxury. Maybe it's a special occasion and you've used vouchers and deals to secure a few nights' break in a luxury hotel, but have booked the cheapest room, and would really love to move up a few floors, yet it's unaffordable. Maybe you'd love to fulfil your partner's dream of turning left on entering a plane and accepting a cool glass of champers rather doubling over in cattle class as usual. What's the solution? An upgrade, of course. But it's not easy: a cheeky grin, smart suit and some light flirtation with the check-in lady is no longer enough. In fact, it's quite likely to get you seated next to the loo instead. 'Flights are full. Airlines are pressured to bring in ancillary revenue which means you'll pay something for not only that upgrade, but also the privilege of boarding early and even that airline meal.' So says Kate Maxwell, very seasoned traveller and editor-in-chief of jetsetter.com, a free, members-only site that provides insider knowledge and deals on holidays. 'But,' she adds, 'it never hurts to try.' Here are her secret upgrade tips:

On a plane:

- Turn up early and ask politely. Ask to be considered for an upgrade and always say please. But don't bother if you're an unlikely candidate – for example, travelling with six kids and a muddy dog, or you purchased your ticket for an extremely low price.

- No luck? Ask again at the gate. The airline won't know exactly what availability it has until everyone has checked in, so ask (politely) if there's any chance of an upgrade here as well. Often there will be a price attached to the upgrade, but this price sometimes decreases if the seats are not purchased at full price. Expect to pay up to about £60 for short-haul and £75 to £250 for a long-haul trip.

- Pick a busy flight. If your flight is overbooked, offer to give up your seat in return for an upgrade – or if you can afford to take the next flight instead, offer to do so on the condition of an upgrade (which may be offered anyway).

- Dress up. It's not going to help as much as it once did, but I can pretty much guarantee you won't be upgraded in a Juicy tracksuit, a tank top and Ugg boots. Channel the glamorous jet-set days of the sixties and put on that frock.

- If you're really keen on flying higher, investigate actually booking business instead of economy. The difference between business and economy is sometimes smaller than you might think – perhaps £150 – so it might be worth paying the difference.

- Think about booking an extra seat. These are not just for the obese! If your flight is dirt cheap this is a way of guaranteeing you get more room – just remember to check in for the second seat and show your boarding pass at the gate, otherwise they might give it to a standby passenger.

- Follow your favourite airlines on social media. You'll be the first to hear about great offers. And look out for sales on business-class flights, when they can be the same price as economy.

At a hotel:

- If you don't ask, you don't get, so always ask for an upgrade. I never check into a hotel without asking for an upgrade to a better room. Large hotel chains such as Starwood have loyalty schemes too, but they're not as prevalent as those run by airlines, and you're much more likely to be upgraded at a hotel than on a flight. The chains want you to come back, and if they have a better room that's going to lie empty otherwise, the chances are they'll put you in it. In fact some hotels do it as a matter of course (and so they should!).

- Bigger is not always better. The obvious request is 'May I be upgraded to a bigger room or a suite?' But if you are travelling to a major city with lots of street noise, London or New York for example, I'd take a normal room on the 31st floor over a suite on the 2nd floor any day – and twice on Sundays (because I get to sleep in). Make sure you request a room on a high floor, along with your request for a suite.

- If it's your birthday, honeymoon or anniversary, let the hotel know. I'd never recommend lying about this (although you'd be surprised how many people do) but if it really is a special occasion, tell them, and wait for the champagne to flow . . .

- The longer you stay, the less you pay. Hotels often offer incentives for staying longer – four nights for the price of three; free spa treatments; meals or drinks in the bar.

- Travel during the week for the best deals. Rooms, apart from in business hubs, tend to be considerably cheaper during the week.

- Choose a new hotel. A hotel that's still establishing itself is more likely to upgrade you based on availability because it'll want to give a good impression – and chances are it'll have more available rooms.

- Check in after 2 p.m. After the standard 2 p.m. check-in time, hotels will know which rooms remain unallocated.

If your trip is flexible, try to travel at the cheapest times – so rule out school holidays (usually the third week of July to the end of August, a late week in October, mid December to early January, a week in the middle of February and a fortnight in April, but if in doubt check a local school's website) and, if possible, weekends. The cheapest period to fly is usually Tuesday to Tuesday, and the middle of the day is normally cheaper than early evening. Skyscanner.net has a nifty graph tool which allows you to compare fares across a whole month or year so you can find the very cheapest day to fly.

If you can also be flexible about your departure or arrival airport, look at the various options, as it may cost less to fly to or from a base a little further out of town. Make sure it's convenient, though: if you're forced to book a cab to transport you from MiddleofNowhere Airport to the centre of town, it could end up being more expensive.

Another flight cost-cutter is taking the indirect route. If saving money is a higher priority than speed, stop-over flights tend to be cheaper. Flight-comparison sites momondo. com, kayak.co.uk, travelocity.co.uk, travelsupermarket. com, plus the aforementioned skyscanner.net, will all allow you to look at the option of mixing flights from different carriers with budget airlines, which can work out cheaper.

Want a flight to a popular destination? If your holiday is to Faliraki rather than French Polynesia, or Marbella rather than Mauritius, you might be able to nab a spare seat on a charter flight. These are put on by package holiday firms for their own customers, but if there's any extra room the seats often go cheap. Sometimes they are listed on the above comparison sites, but it's worth looking direct on the likes of thomson.co.uk as well as via specialist search engines like charterflights.co.uk.

For popular destinations, it's also worth checking out lastminute.com's secret flight checker – the same deal as the secret hotels idea, described above, but it's even easier to work out the operator because it tells you the rough arrival and departure times, airports and any stop-overs, and there usually aren't that many options: tinyurl.com/secretflights.

Avoiding baggage charges

Budget airlines make extensive profits from passengers deigning to take some possessions with them on holiday. But these costs can be avoided. I once flew to Spain for a week with just hand luggage, and had enough clothes to wear a different outfit every day. I did it like this: just before check-in, I went to the airport loo and put on lots of extra clothes. So my legs wore leggings, skinny jeans, baggy jeans and hosted two jumpers tied around my waist. I wore four T-shirts and popped another jumper on top, then looped one around my shoulders. The rest of my baggage easily slipped into a rucksack, where I also stored a large carrier bag. And yes, I had some funny looks when I got on the plane, sat down and immediately started taking off my trousers . . . and then another two pairs . . . but by then, there were no extra baggage fees to contend with and I could just decant my clothes into my spare carrier bag.

Nowadays some canny manufacturers have come up with easier ways to cram as much on to your person as possible: so-called wearable luggage. I'll admit that I haven't yet tried it, but the concept of the Jaktogo definitely sounds ingenious. It looks like a normal bag but can be unfolded and worn during check-in and boarding, then switched back to a bag once you're on board. It comes in three different versions – jacket, dress and poncho – and three different sizes (large, extra large and extra-extra large) starting from €70, and in black, denim or leather. Sure, you won't win any fashion competitions, but if it wins you big savings, think what fashion you could spend it on . . . The Jaktogo's maker claims its fourteen pockets can hold up to thirty pounds, but 'you probably wouldn't want to wear it for more than five minutes.' (See jaktogo.com.)

Other ideas include using the lightest possible luggage to cram the most amount of stuff in your case. The £25 Cabin Max bag, for example, is designed to fit the maximum airline carry-on luggage dimensions of 55 x 40 x 20cm, and contains 44 litres of space inside. Whether travelling on a budget jet or traditional carrier, remember to weigh your luggage before leaving home – if it tots up to more than the airline's limit, strip some stuff out to avoid paying extra charges.

Ferry

Avoiding the hours of hanging around for check-in and security at airports means that travelling by ferry can be a lot less stressful than flying, particularly for families. For those wanting to drive abroad, taking a ferry also makes it easier to carry more stuff, and can be significantly cheaper. But you have to plan ahead. I was flabbergasted at a recent quote for a last-minute ferry from Poole, on the south coast of England, to Cherbourg in France – in the end, it worked out cheaper to fly and hire a car. My big mistake was to try to book last minute: ferry tickets are far cheaper in advance, particularly more than twenty-eight days in advance.

Look up the journey options on a ferry aggregator site such as ferrysavers.com or aferry.co.uk. They're great for finding out who operates particular routes and how much cheaper they are at particular times of the day, week or year, but when actually booking, you may get a better price by going direct to the operator, where there are less likely to be agency or bookings fees.

Across the Channel, sailing during the night tends to be far cheaper, whilst weekday crossings – especially on Tuesdays, Wednesdays and Thursdays – are cheaper than weekend ones. Again, the school holiday period is more expensive. Find all the ports near to your destination to help you track down the nearest (saving petrol) as well as the cheapest. You may need to decide whether saving money or time is more important. And find out about your journey options too: high-speed ferries and hovercrafts are usually more expensive than slower ones. Most major ferry routes charge for one car plus up to five passengers, so if you haven't filled up your car, you're wasting money. Advertise your space on a car-pooling site like blablacar.com or liftshare.com (see page 206) or ask friends and family if they know of any people looking for a ride. Sharing the ferry cost will slash the total transport bill.

Frequent cross-Channel ferry users should sign up for company loyalty cards, which offer discounts off journeys, as well as investing in multi-ticket deals. DFDS Seaways, for example, offers twelve or more return trips from £19 per car each way. Overnight options – such as the 'Dutch Flyer' train and ferry service from London or any Greater

Anglia rail station to Amsterdam or any Dutch station, which costs from £69 one way for a single berth cabin with shower, toilet, satellite TV and free Wi-Fi – may save the cost of one night's accommodation as well as costing less than flying.

Train

If you, like me, find buying train tickets in Britain confusing (I was once so engrossed in reading a book on a train platform that I missed my once-an-hour train; annoying enough, but doubly so when I tried to get on the next train, only to be told my ticket was no longer valid. Most expensive book I ever bought.), then take a deep breath before attempting the same in Europe.

Luckily, here we have top advice from Mark Smith, a career railwayman who now runs the train travel site seat61.com. The website is always my first stop when looking for train deals around the UK or abroad – frankly, there's boffin-level detail laid out very clearly, which means you'll never pay more than necessary. Here, Smith reveals his top tips on tracking down the cheapest ticket prices.

'Taking a high-speed train is a great way to get from the UK, not just to Paris or Brussels, but to Switzerland, Germany, the South of France, or (using a sleeper train) to Spain, Italy, Austria or Prague. It's the greener option, emitting up to ninety per cent less carbon dioxide per passenger than a flight. And now European train operators are finally offering airline-style budget fares. London to Paris starts at £39 one way, or £69 return, on the Eurostar, and a ticket from Paris to Geneva or Zurich in Switzerland by high-speed train can be added from €25 each way. Or a couchette on the 'Thello' overnight sleeper to Venice can be added from €35 each way. And with trains there are no booking fees, baggage fees, check-in fees or fuel surcharges, as airlines charge. As the train takes you from city centre to city centre you also save the cost of travelling to and from remote airports.

'How to secure the best deals? Booking online, direct with the operator is usually the cheapest option. You can use the following websites to book trains within the country in question, and international trains starting in that country. They all have an English-language version:

- FRANCE: tgv-europe.com (look for cheap 'prems' fares between French cities; Paris to Nice from €25)

- SWITZERLAND: sbb.ch

- ITALY: trenitalia.com (look for cheap 'mini' fares from just €9 between major Italian cities, and 'smart' fares to neighbouring countries)

- GERMANY: bahn.de (look for 'savings' fares from just €19 within Germany and to or from neighbouring countries)

- AUSTRIA: oebb.at (this can book sleeper trains from Austria to Italy from €39 and daytime trains from Vienna to Prague or Budapest from €19)

- SPAIN: renfe.com (look for cheap 'web' fares between Spanish cities; Madrid to Seville from €33)

- PORTUGAL: cp.pt (the international sleeper train between

Lisbon and Madrid can be booked at renfe.com)

- SWEDEN: sj.se (this can also book trains from Copenhagen to Stockholm)

- CZECH REPUBLIC: cd.cz/eshop (this can book tickets from Prague to Vienna, Budapest and Bratislava from just €19)

'Some international train services have their own websites:

- Eurostar: high-speed trains from London to Paris and Brussels (eurostar.com)

- Thalys: high-speed trains Paris–Brussels–Amsterdam and Cologne (thalys.com)

- Thello: sleeper trains from Paris to Milan, Verona and Venice (thello.com)

- City Night Line sleeper trains from Paris to Berlin, Munich and Hamburg, and from Amsterdam to Zurich, Munich, Prague, Copenhagen and Warsaw can be booked at the German railways website bahn.de

'Now, on to strategies to find the cheapest tickets. First: book early. Booking normally opens ninety days ahead, and the sooner you book, the cheaper it is likely to be. You're more likely to find cheap tickets midweek than on busy Fridays or Sunday afternoons. Eurostar can be booked up to 120 days ahead, but if you're going beyond Paris or Brussels it's best to wait and book all your tickets together.

'Sleeper trains: remember these save an expensive hotel bill, as long as you book a couchette or sleeper so you can get a good night's sleep! Paris to Venice from €35 with couchette (thello.com); Amsterdam to Prague or Copenhagen from €59 with couchette.

'Railpasses: an InterRail pass (for European residents) or Eurail pass (for overseas visitors) can save money over expensive full-price fares, and give you freedom to move around spontaneously as the mood grabs you. But don't assume it's the cheapest option until you've checked what normal tickets would cost, especially if you are willing to book a cheap 'budget' train fare in advance.'

Holiday money

Track exchange rates on a site like Travelex's Rate Tracker, travelex.co.uk, and use the data to work out which country is most affordable. When the dollar is weak, it's not only the US that will become more affordable, but countries with linked currencies like South and Central America, and parts of the Caribbean that are already cheaper and will become more so.

Don't pay over the odds for holiday money. For the sake of security, you should travel abroad with cash (you'll usually need it to get out of the airport, train station, ferry port, etc.) as well as cards – to avoid the security risk of holding a chunk of cash – but opt for the right ones to cut costs. When withdrawing foreign currency in the UK, opt for a provider that doesn't charge commission (such as Marks & Spencer or the Post Office) and check you're getting good rates. It's easy to compare the options – tap in how much you want at travelmoneymax.com and it will do it for you. The savings mount up: converting £1,000 into euros at an airport (where the worst rates are usually charged, as they know most travellers will have no choice but to use them) could involve paying as much as £100 more than using the best currency bureau. Many of these are online. Take care and don't convert too much cash in any one single bureau: currency companies don't have any compensation protection, so if they collapse, you could lose your money.

It's a good idea to take some plastic to use for spending overseas too, but be careful which one you pick: your everyday low-interest or high cashback card may be the most expensive one to use abroad. Most credit cards add a loading fee of three per cent to the exchange rates, and charge extra for withdrawals from cash machines abroad as well as interest on the amount withdrawn from the day that it is taken out of the ATM – even if you pay off your bill in full.

But there are usually a couple of cards on the market – such as Santander's Zero card or Halifax's Clarity – that do not charge fees on spending or taking money out of a hole in the wall, so shop around and do so well before you take off: a new card can take as long as a month to drop on your doorstep.

Debit cards can be problematic too: some banks impose fees of up to £1.50 each time a debit card is used to buy anything, and then take a cut of the total spending bill too. If you need to use an expensive one whilst overseas, remember it will work out cheaper to withdraw larger sums so you're charged fees less often – but again, try to avoid walking around with a lot of cash.

Another alternative is a pre-paid currency card, which you load up with cash ahead of your holiday. You can still use the card to pay via chip and PIN but, as they're not linked to your bank account, some view them as more secure for use overseas. Opt for one without spending fees. The big names offering these include Travelex's Cash Passport, FairFX, and Caxton FX.

Car hire

Before going through all the hassle of hiring a car, make sure you really need one. In major cities, public transport is often faster – and cheaper – for getting around, and you avoid the problem of parking. Research your destination first – when I travelled around Costa Rica, I found roads like ploughed fields and signage so poor that foreigners in hire cars could barely get around. Instead, I stuck to the very cheap public buses (average price: £2 for a cross-country journey). There were downsides: the official timetable posters were years out of date. My solution was to ask five different local people, take an average, and get to the bus stop early.

If you do need a car, plan in advance for as many circumstances as possible to get the cheapest rate. For example, adding a second driver to the insurance policy usually costs far more if you turn up and make the request than if you had booked it in advance. Some local providers – and, usually, the international brand Sixt, although it can vary from location to location – include two drivers on the policy as standard, but the vast majority do not.

To find the cheapest provider, the first step, as usual, should be an online comparison site; they seem to be the UK's internet specialism. Moneymaxim.co.uk and carrentals.co.uk both have reliable comparison engines. If you find a decent deal, book it via a cashback website – this usually provides at least £50 back for a week or so's hire.

But before doing so, it's worth checking these quotes from comparison sites – which usually focus on the big, international brands – against those of providers that are local to your destination. To find out which are best, ask a local contact, phone your hotel concierge or receptionist and search on recommendation sites. This will obviously be much easier if the country has English as its mother tongue, or you're fluent in Gujurati (if going to India – it's probably less useful in Mongolia).

Anyone booking a rental car in America, even a six-foot bean pole who won't set foot in a car that's smaller than a Ford Mondeo, should consider booking the most compact car on offer. There's so little demand for compact cars in the US that most rental places don't even stock them – meaning you'll automatically be upgraded, but still pay the cheapest price.

When it comes to picking up the car, it's always worth haggling. You probably won't be able to get the car rental price down, but may be able to nab free hire of satnav, a couple of days' extra for a limited fee, airport drop off or a similar extra.

Lastly, a quick – but valuable – word on insurance. The first time I hired a car, in Portugal a few years ago, I turned up at the counter and stood in line feeling super-smug about my rental quote. I'd booked online and secured what I thought was a steal of a deal, a feeling which only grew as I inched up the queue and heard what other people were putting on their credit cards. Then I got to the front and discovered the excess that came with the cover I'd booked was €1,000. I was to be driving up rock-strewn country roads across the middle of Portugal, and there was a very strong likelihood of chipped paint or one of the other minor problems that car hire companies capitalise on. So I could do nothing but swallow an eye-watering €300 charge to wipe out the 'excess'. And obliterate any feelings of smugness.

Being a money-saving nerd, one of the first things I did once I'd got home and put the holiday washing in the machine was to work out if there was a way to avoid this in the future. Luckily, there is: some insurers offer stand-alone excess-protection policies for car hire, which are seriously cheap in comparison. Providers include protectyourbubble. com and carhireexcess.com. Moneymaxim has a useful comparison tool to help you find them. Just click 'compare car hire insurance', then 'car hire excess insurance'. You can opt either to buy an annual policy, or just enough cover for a single holiday. A year's cover in Europe for a forty-year-old costs about £40.

Extra holiday money-savers

- **Stay put.** Yup, sometimes you want to go abroad for a week or two and no recession is going to put a stop to it. But sometimes all you're really craving is a week away from work or your normal routine. So stay at home and fill up your week with all the things you don't normally have the time to do, like dining with friends, going on day trips, and exploring your local area. Unplug the phone, switch off your BlackBerry, log out of your email and spend some of the money you're saving on *not* travelling on your favourite meals, trips to a spa, local beauty spots, DVDs, music and other ways you like to enjoy yourself.

- **Get on your bike.** It's cheap or can even be free to take your bike on a ferry, and you'll save on transport costs when you get there. Think about the hill gradient though: unless the Tour de France is your idea of a great holiday, you might want to pick flat Holland or Belgium over the Alps. Find European cycle routes at eurovelo.org.

- **Find the local cheap hotel chains.** Most Western countries have local equivalents of Premier Inn and Travelodge – cheap, no-frills, clean rooms that you can rely on. In Europe, Ibis, Mercure, and Campanile offer a similar deal. If you're travelling elsewhere, ask locals, or crowdsource via Twitter or Facebook to work out the best-value chains.

- **Read all about it.** In the months leading up to summer, most of Britain's newspapers start offering holiday tokens for discounted breaks.

- **Ensure your passport is valid well ahead of time.** Otherwise you'll have to waste extra pounds on a rushed application – pounds which you could spend on holiday.

- **Check out guidebooks from the library rather than buying new ones.** Ask for an extra-long loan period to avoid facing fines on your return – it might not be your priority when there's all that unpacking to do.

- **Check out hotel lobbies for tourist magazines:** these often contain discount codes.

- **Plan your time in advance** – I usually do this whilst travelling on aeroplanes, trains etc. – because museums and attractions often offer free entrance at certain times (e.g. New York's MOMA is free on Friday nights). Look out, too, for free festivals and events.

- **Book airport parking ahead of time.** Never just turn up at Heathrow or one of its rivals and expect to park without shelling out the equivalent of a night or more in a hotel. Instead, book in advance. Britain's biggest airports, including Heathrow and Gatwick, often run parking deals at its on-site multi-storeys for those who book ahead. I recently used one at Gatwick and parked just a minute's walk from the airport exit for a week for £35. Off-site car parks, run by independent operators, are usually cheaper but involve more hassle, including waiting for a shuttle, so you'll need to allow more time. Sometimes car insurers or breakdown cover providers offer special deals. Airport hotels also offer one-night stays before flights that include long-term parking in the cost.

- **Before arriving at your destination, research the transport options.** Cab journeys between your hotel and the airport can quickly add up, but if you arrive in a new country unprepared they may seem like the only option. So take a few minutes to look up local shuttle services, buses and train options, including how long they take, where they depart from and how much they cost, in guide books or online before departure.

- **Be careful of your mobile phone costs** when abroad – see page 245.

- **Eat like a local.** Veering off the beaten track will help you avoid tourist-trap restaurants and find the places that locals go to eat. Do your research ahead of time – browse food blogs for your destination, ask people on Twitter (guidebooks can be good, but sometimes by the time off-the-beaten-track places make it into print, the owner catches wind and hikes the prices), and ask people who've been to your destination recently for recommendations. When you're there, ask locals for their favourite eateries. Best to steer clear of people like hotel receptionists – they may be compelled to recommend the owner's friend's place next door – but get chatting to people in shops, on public transport, on the plane, in the loo – anywhere, really – and ask for their favourite places to eat. Going local will be much cheaper than spending an evening at a place where the menu is translated into fifteen languages, and be a far better holiday experience, whether you come across a local French café baking its own croissants or Hong Kong's best street food seller offering mouth-watering bowls of HK$1 noodles.

- **The only exception to the above rule?** The hotel breakfast buffet. If you're paying more to stay in a plush hotel, it would simply be rude not to avail oneself of a delicious bread roll and cheese sandwich, plus banana and apple, for lunch. Well that's what I tell myself as I bring in an oversized beach bag to breakfast and discreetly wrap up a roll in a napkin . . .

- **If you're not staying at a place with inclusive breakfast** (or it's just a bowl of cornflakes, which frankly isn't very portable) check out local supermarkets for lunch. My fiancé and I have spent many a lunchtime picnicking on supermarket or deli-bought bread, cheese, meat or a dip like houmous, and cherry tomatoes plus fruit, crisps and chocolate. It not only means you can eat exactly what you want (and have a cheap snack ready for that tourist-o'clock feeling when your legs start to drag late in the day) but you also save money which you can splurge at dinner time instead.

- **The supermarket food rule is especially true on skiing holidays.** On my last trip to the Alps, even ropey-looking slope-side cafés were selling a stingy portion of chips (made of plain old potato, not platinum) for a whopping €7. I figure this is why skiing jackets have so many pockets. Fill 'em up with snacks, plonk yourself down in a safe place on a mountain and there you have it: a cheap meal with a free view.

- **Another money-saving skiing tip: never hire your equipment when you arrive at the resort** – instead, reserve it first online. You'll save a bomb, and will be hiring the exact same kit, often from the very same shop you'd have strolled into anyway. I rented skis, poles and boots for a week in Morzine, France for €70 from Intersport, a big brand chain situated plonk in the middle of the resort, using the website alpinresorts. com. The boots were personally fitted to me at the shop, and all the customer service was the same as usual (which was not great, because I was in France, but still) but, as I'd booked in advance, I saved more than thirty per cent on the walk-in price. It's easy to do: just tap in the name of your ski resort, the type of skis you want, plus your shoe size, and the site will offer prices at a range of rental shops in different locations around the slopes. Brands on offer include Saloman, Rossignol and Burton.

- **Get paid to travel.** And not just if you're an international travelling salesman. Even if the furthest your employer has ever sent you is to the local newsagent to pick up a pint of milk for the tea-round, it's still possible to entirely fund a trip abroad (and even earn money whilst there to boost your savings at home) with a working holiday. Anyone with experience working with kids might be able to score a job working at a summer camp in somewhere like the US, Asia, Australia or New Zealand. Most are run during the long summer holidays. For more details check out a major scheme-organiser like Bunac (bunac. org/uk). To work at a camp based in the US, most staff have to pay about £500 for flights, insurance, food and accommodation, but then pocket salaries of around £450–£800 for working two months of summer. It may not be a huge profit at the end, but since return flights are covered, you'll still have about £300 for more travelling.

- **Other kinds of temporary jobs abroad include farming.** Wannabe farmers might enjoy cattle work in the outback; the Australian Job Search has details here: jobsearch.gov.au/harvesttrail – or just pick a country and look for casual work whilst there or hunt down a more organised scheme before heading out.

Visiting Mickey Mouse

A special word on Disney holidays in the US. When the kids (or your soppy Pocahontas-loving other half) succeed in convincing you that now is the time to visit a Disney theme park, your wallet may shudder at the thought of its upcoming eons of emptiness. Theme parks are expensive; so too are the meals, parking, hotels, travel, and mouse-ear-shaped headband you'll undoubtedly need to buy to remember the experience. But if you're planning a Disney break, there's one website you need to visit, and explore in forensic detail: mousesavers.com. It has exhaustive knowledge on not only the best Disney ticket deals but the most convenient hotels, cheapest parking, queue-beating secrets, how to save on tickets and passes – everything you could want to know, apart from who's really inside that Mickey costume.

Families

And you thought labour was the most painful part of child-rearing. Nope, the most painful part is probably the pocket pain. The cost of raising a child until the age of twenty-one is now a massive £218,024, according to the insurer LV=. That's including more than £60,000 on childcare and babysitting, £18,000 on food, £9,000 on toys, and £3,373 on furniture. You're probably thinking, 'Oh, it's just one of those multiple-choice surveys where parents eagerly click random answers in a bid to get to the end and find out whether they really have been the lucky winner of a three-night holiday in Benidorm.' You're probably thinking, 'I don't spend anything like that – three grand on furniture? Their entire bedroom came from the bargain corner of Ikea.'

And you might be right. But tot up your annual spending on the sweets, nappies, puréed food, vegetables bought to purée into food, Magimixers lost to the puréed-food cause, sleep suits, new-fangled sleep suit bought in the hope that its label claiming 'promotes long sleep' really worked, endless toys played with for less time than their packaging littered the living room, and so on, and you'll find that those precious little darlings who may, or may not, currently be screaming from the naughty step really are a lot more expensive than you'd thought.

Now a lot of the stuff written in this book before the present chapter holds true – or even truer – for families of older kids too. Whether it's for packed lunches, or teenage boys with voracious appetites or for a baby, your food bill will most likely be a large chunk of your household outgoings. Perhaps a bigger home means energy and utility bills cost more too. But there are other, family-focused ways to make and save money whilst bringing up kids – and not just 'use contraception' as many a witty comic suggests . . .

Babes in arms

Believe the ads and you might think your baby was born demanding couture sleeper suits and a mahogany crib. Hardly. Ask parenting friends and relatives who are of the 'never again' school of parenting if you can buy or borrow their kids' hand-me-downs. Many will be happy to clear their loft for a good cause. Borrowing is especially worthwhile for newborns, who will outgrow most of their clothes and early Moses basket, booties, bath tubs etc. in weeks. There's really no need to buy everything new – although be careful with car seats, as some of their safety features depend on their never having been in a crash or dropped, and research also suggests all babies should have new mattresses.

Another way to trim costs right from the start is by buying goods and selling outgrown kit at nearly-new sales. Find one near you run by the National Childbirth Trust at nct.org.uk or look for posters at local schools, nurseries, childcare clinics etc., or log in to babyswaporshop.co.uk. Nope, it doesn't offer sale or return on your babe, but does have pregnancy, baby and parenting items to buy or swap, including cots, feeding equipment, toys, Babygros and stair safety gates. Some are new, some are second-hand, but they're all clearly listed. You can search either by product or look at what's available in your local area.

🖥️ *'New parents-to-be – you'll always feel pressured to buy mountains of kid-care stuff, but as a father of four, I can promise you half of it is totally unnecessary! Talk to other parents for advice – and as for gifts from well-wishers, ask for fewer teddies and more Babygro vests.'* – MARK, NORTHAMPTON

For expensive items like a cot or car seat that you might want or need to have new, consider asking family or friends to help out with the purchase rather than buying you presents like pretty Babygros that aren't essential. And to budget baby expenses, the government-run Money Advice Service has a useful interactive costs calculator which helps new parents work out where costs for essentials mount up, and where extras can be cut out (see tinyurl.com/babycostcalc).

Even nappies don't have to be money down the drain. Or not as much, anyway. 'The average baby uses more than 4,000 nappies in their young life,' points out Kate Moore, head of savings at Family Investments. 'Non-disposable nappies tend to work out as more cost-effective – and some councils offer money-off vouchers on purchasing non-disposable nappies.' Contact your council or, in the capital, look up the Real Nappies for London scheme. Some – like

Hackney in east London – also offer a laundry service where they pick them up from your home every week (see hackneyrealnappy.net). If disposables are a must, bulk-buy packs whenever they're on offer.

Sign up to parenting clubs too. Asia, an aunt of two kids from Surrey, says her family has saved hundreds thanks to these. 'Join as many parenting groups run by retailers as possible for freebies and discounts,' she says. 'Tesco, Boots and Mothercare will send you free stuff all the time as well as money-off vouchers for nappies, clothes and other baby essentials.' As an example, Boots Parenting Club gives out money-off vouchers, extra Boots Clubcard points and free gifts like a changing bag; the Bounty Parenting Club includes discounts and free packs of Pampers; whilst Sainsbury's Little Ones club offers a Huggies baby bundle including toiletries and a changing mat. Asia's other tips to new parents are: 'Always accept hand-me-downs from friends and family – you might think that you always have enough clothes but you will be surprised as to how quickly kids grow out of things. And always keep snacks with you: it's more than likely that as soon as you step out of the house, kids will say they're hungry for snacks and drinks. Rather than giving in and spending pounds in the local shops, dip into the snacks you've got with you.'

Kids

You know those unwanted games/DVDs/albums/books/gadgets/collectables/pieces of junk that your kids spent two weeks begging you for just a month ago? Palm it off on to some other kid who's still desperate for it – and get something in return. That's what parents and kids can do at swapping site swapit.co.uk. Users earn virtual currency 'swapits' for every item they pass on to someone else, and can also earn swapits from completing research surveys and eating healthy food at school. Obviously parents will need to check they're happy with the activities on the site, but they're all aimed at kids who bank their swapits and can then spend them on a wide range of new and second-hand items on the site. Items are all dispatched via the central Swapit address for the sake of safety.

Don't forget just how good homemade and old-fashioned toys and games can be. Make your own play dough by mixing half a cup of hot water with one cup of flour, half a cup of salt, a tablespoon of oil and any colour of food dye. Obviously it can't be played with until it has cooled down, but the whole making process only takes about five minutes.

If you're imaginative enough to start a game, kids will happily play with things as simple as cardboard boxes for hours. Testing this out on my young nieces, I got three hours' worth of play out of two former John Lewis packing boxes – first encouraging them to transform them into a car using craft materials and crayons, then giving them characters with jobs to carry out – driving around the motorway, picking up cargo, etc. Other rainy-day ideas like musical statues – play music while the kids dance around, then ask them to freeze when the music stops; or building a den using a sheet, boxes and chairs; and the perennial parents' favourite, sleeping lions, are always a hit. Download and print off colouring sheets from the likes of crayola.com. Outside, in local park playgrounds, games of tag, dodgeball, tennis and football are easy, free ways to fill time. For more ideas, see playgroundfun.org.uk and nhs.uk/Change4Life.

Buy second-hand toys from local car boot sales and websites like eBay. A box of used Lego and other branded toys can be purchased for a fraction of the price and can easily be washed before being handed over to the kids. And since more often than not, children will beg for *that* new toy for months but play with it for minutes, the rental service from toyboxlive.co.uk might be of interest. It isn't cheap, but it might save money for parents who seriously spoil their kids. For a monthly fee of £24.99, parents can choose up to four toys at a time, which will be delivered straight to the door. Once the children have had enough of the four toys, they can send them back and have new ones delivered. It caters for children aged from newborn to five-plus, with brands including Fisher Price, Hippy Chick, Tomy and Wallaboo.

For school clothes, don't immediately rush out and buy new: most schools run bring-and-buy sales which may be an easier way to swap toys, clothes, uniforms and more. If there's no class-wide uniform sale, join up with other parents of children who are older and younger than your own and set up a clothes swap. If you do want to buy new, it's often cheaper to mix and match generic school clothes, like plain pinafores, skirts, trousers and shirts that can be bought from local shops, with one or two school-branded sweatshirts or jumpers. And if there's even a tiny chance that the little darling will have a new sibling one day, don't chuck anything out yet – shove it in a corner, loft, under a bed or in a parental abode – by the time it's Junior-number-two's turn to start school, he or she will never remember that the smart 'new' uniform is a hand-me-down.

For bargainous days out, use group-buying sites (see page 24), take a trip to the local library for free books and reading groups, and use local leisure centres for a swim or other sports session for a couple of quid. Picnics in country parks or on beaches are a great cheap day out, as are some of the hundreds of free museums and galleries around the country, including many of Britain's best, like the Science Museum, National Portrait Gallery, Imperial War Museum, British Museum in London, the Tate in Liverpool, Swansea Museum and the National Museum of Scotland – which all have free entry.

Find other free days out and activities at the dofreestuff. com website. Anyone travelling to an attraction by train should find out whether two-for-one entry is available via the daysoutguide.co.uk website. It has BOGOF deals on a huge range of attractions including Kew Gardens, the Wimbledon Lawn Tennis Museum, Chelsea FC tours, Alton Towers theme park, Bournemouth Aviation Museum, West End shows and more. Don't forget to use the usual money-saving days out ideas too, be that for cinema, theatre or TV recordings (see page 36) or meals out (page 141). During August, kids can also go free to West End shows if they are accompanied by an adult paying full price – see kidsweek.co.uk.

Presents

Set up a present cupboard or basket so that next time you're approaching the school gates and remember that afternoon is Nigel's fourth birthday party, instead of having to dash into a posh toy shop to buy a £20 train set for a little boy you're not quite sure you or your offspring could actually identify, you can open your present cupboard and whip out the £6 train set you bought in the sales. Keep the cupboard full of potential presents that you buy whenever you see something nice that's good value.

This goes for grown-up gifts too – a stash of little chocolates and toiletries on 'buy one, get one free' can easily be bundled together in cellophane and tied with ribbon to dazzle recipients with a pricey-looking but bargainous gift. Of course, you'll also use your present cupboard to dump unwanted prezzies for that time-old recycling initiative known as 're-gifting'. Be careful, though. A few years ago I had to carefully rearrange my face as I unwrapped a photo-frame set from a friend that I'd given to her a year before. Shove a notebook in the cupboard to jot down who gave you said unwanted gift and when, to make sure you don't send it right back to them, or anyone who was around to see it entering your hands . . .

'I look in charity shops for games for the grandchildren – there are very good bargains there. I've bought Monopoly, Junior Scrabble and alphabet games, sometimes for as little as a pound.' – RONALD, RICHMOND

Making money off your kids

We're not talking child labour here, but your kids don't have to be exclusively revenue-suckers. Spend five minutes checking your benefit entitlements – including tax credits and child benefit – and it could help bring in vital extra cash or savings. And, if applicable, sign up to workplace childcare voucher schemes, which are open to all working parents – regardless of income – of kids up to the age of fifteen. They allow you to pay for childcare from pre-tax income, meaning it's exempt from tax and national insurance, so the savings quickly mount up. Find out about eligibility – and prompt your employer to sign up if they haven't already – at hmrc.gov.uk/childcare and work out the benefits at computersharevoucherservices.com.

Once your kids are old enough, encourage them to get a job before or after school or on weekends. It'll be good for them – and your finances – if they start saving up for their own treats rather than badgering you for them. Popular ideas include newspaper deliveries, babysitting, tutoring, car-washing, sports-coaching, lawn-mowing, dog-walking, or even starting their own business.

Exercise

I blame muscly Madonna and skinny-minny celebrities for coming along and convincing us that the (expensive, time-consuming, smelly) gym is *the* place to go and do exercise. OK, I've heard there are some people who love the gym. I may have even been one of them for about two days, before I realised that 'going to the gym' meant moving beyond my routine of hanging around in the fruit juice bar, a three-minute jogging session, then a sauna and jacuzzi session. It might be obvious that I don't like the gym. But even if you do, the sight of many more pounds falling out of your bank account each month than off your waistline can be depressing.

Gyms are famous for sucking new members in – usually at the start of January, when Britons' intentions are purer than pure – with cut-price deals, then making it harder to give up the monthly subscription than to quit smoking. In fact, one case recently came to light of a seven-months pregnant gym member whose husband had lost his job, leaving the couple living on state benefits and forced to move home to a place twelve miles away from their nearest gym. The gym-goer asked the chain to reconsider the two-year verbal contract they had agreed. Instead, the gym insisted the couple pay £780 to be released from the contract – until a newspaper and Twitter went to war against the gym chain and shamed it into reversing its decision. Luckily, there are ways to do battle with the fat cells without stepping near a direct debit form, which I'll describe in a second.

But first, if you're one of those types who loves the gym, there's almost certainly a way you can pay less for it. If you live near a city centre with tons of gyms, for example, it's likely that you'll be able to get at least a month's free membership by signing up to their free trials and vouchers. I know, because I once spent three months doing just that with the help of a local café that kept giving out free day passes to my local gym. (I used them purely for a swim and sauna, but still.)

To find the freebies, just check out the websites of national chains such as Fitness First – it frequently offers free seven-day passes (fitnessfirst.co.uk/weekjanuary); LA Fitness – more often three-day passes (lafitness.co.uk); Nuffield Health (nuffieldhealth.com), which usually has free day passes up for grabs; Esporta (esporta.com), again day passes; and Virgin Active (virginactive.co.uk) – likewise, usually free day passes. Or free-gym-pass.co.uk lists gym freebies available at any particular point in time. Ask your friends if they have offers, too; most gyms shower members with free passes (not literally – that could lead to paper cuts) in a bid to lure new bodies on board.

My local council-run swimming pool has a gym on top of it that was renovated in Britain's boom years. What that actually means is that, with its treadmills, flat-screen TVs and fun gym equipment, like weighted hula hoops, it's actually better equipped than some of the run-down private gyms in my area. And it only costs a few quid per visit, where private gyms usually charge at least £20 for a day pass.

Other gym options include payasugym.com, which

has reduced day passes for nearly 300 gyms across the country, and lists no-frills gyms. These are run on the same basis as a budget airline: only the basics are there (no inclusive fluffy towels), but if you are a serious weightlifter, treadmill-runner or other type of gym-based fitness fanatic, that might be all you need. Chains following this formula include the Gym Group (thegymgroup.com), which costs from £16 a month with no contract, so you can cancel whenever you want, and opens its gyms for twenty-four hours, just in case a 2 a.m. indoor rowing session takes your fancy. Others are Pure Gym (puregym.com) and FitSpace (fitspacegyms.co.uk).

Be aware that most gyms also offer cheaper membership for off-peak fitness fans, so if you reckon you'll mostly want to use the gym midweek, find out about the full range of memberships that could help you save money. Think about the location too – if you work in a less wealthy area than you live, for example, or vice versa, you might find the fees cost less in the cheaper zone. Ask if your workplace has a deal with a local gym – corporate agreements can mean cheaper deals. If you go direct, always, always haggle. Gym contracts are often priced in a confusing way, with monthly fees, sign-up charges and sometimes extras like locker fees, towel rental costs, or charges for attending fitness classes too. Know what you're signing up to, for how long, and if it's possible to break the contract at any point, then treat the deal as if you're buying a car from a salesman. Make clear your interest, but be prepared to walk away – doing so will almost always lead to a price reduction, or a few months' free membership.

Free exercise

You don't need to burn money to burn fat. Run around the park – it's free. Get off the bus or train a stop or more before you need to – the journey might cost less, and you're building exercise into your routine. Buying a bike can be a worthwhile investment, especially if your commute is manageable by bike – think how much you'll save on your daily fares (see page 193 on cycling.) A personal trainer might work out cheaper than the gym, too, especially if you group together with, say, four friends and share one trainer. That way, even somewhere like London you can get the cost of a personal trainer down below £10 an hour. Or ask friends or colleagues if they're interested in starting up a weekly football, netball, tennis or other sporting game.

'Cycle to work rather than joining the gym.' – JOANNE, LIVERPOOL

British Military Fitness, the park-based regimes run by ex-army muscle, offers free trial sessions (britmilfit.com) and so does women-only gym-class chain Curves (curves.co.uk). If you're good at self-motivation, buy a fitness DVD (my friends swear by Davina McCall's exercise tapes – fun and not too annoying, apparently).

Or just watch and join in with one of the zillions of free exercise videos on YouTube. Extra bonus: you can do it in your bedroom far away from laughing eyes. A friend and I tried out a yoga session at a local community centre (these, like church halls, can also be an excellent source of cheap exercise classes – ask around your local area) and realised, about fifteen seconds into the hour-long session, that everyone else was more flexible than a prima ballerina and we were as bendy as twigs. The next week, we saved our fivers and logged on to a free yoga tutorial on YouTube instead.

If you're less self-conscious about looking a bit odd in public, some local parks have set up outdoor gyms with fitness bars, trampolines and other gizmos that are all free to use. So too are a lot of local tennis and basketball courts. Other cheap ways to get fit include – for non-parents – borrowing some kids for the day and trying to keep up with them, swapping lifts and escalators for the stairs, doing gardening, going dancing and swimming in the sea, lakes, or – more likely – public lidos (they cost as little as £1 to get into during off-peak sessions – and the backs of cereal packs often have free swimming tickets). It's pretty easy to create a DIY version of a gym-style workout too, for example using cans of baked beans as dumb-bells, holding them in the palms of your hands with arms bent at the elbow, and lifting them up towards your shoulders. Or pile up books or telephone directories in front of the TV and spend the duration of an episode of your favourite goggle-box show climbing up and down like a StairMaster. But if you're not used to exercise, seek advice before launching into the baked-bean dumb-bell routine to avoid causing yourself injury.

I've been impressed by exercise.com, a website with thousands of at-home fitness ideas that you can build together into a workout, including making a fitness programme and, if you're that way inclined, meal journals, and most of the site is free.

'I save money by not using my car very much – which is helped by the fact that I hate driving and get lost frequently. Instead I use my [free transport for pensioners] Freedom Pass which is very useful, and I walk a lot more than I used to, through parks or the woods near me or interesting streets. I like looking at the decor in the different houses and I think it keeps me fitter.' – GILLIAN, LONDON

PART 2
Milking it

SOMEHOW I FIND IT A LOT EASIER to spend time on cutting the cost of nights out and holidays than I do on the boring stuff like filling up the fridge every week or getting to work and back. There's an instant incentive – it's far more fun to research best-value beach resorts than it is to stand in Tesco comparing the cost-per-kg of own-brand and Birds Eye frozen peas. You might get frostbite. But more pertinently, sometimes the potential pennies of savings just don't seem worthwhile. Other things, like the cost of my daily commute, tot up to a massive bill so depressing that I would rather stuff a beanbag than think about it. The thought pattern goes something like, 'I have to get to work every day; it's a horrible, stuffy, packed journey and they still insist I pay £7 a day to do so? I'll file that one away as "unavoidable cost".'

But once every few months I force myself to think about these everyday, boring costs that can take up a huge chunk of annual spending. Because if I didn't, I'd never end up using all the oddities that fill up the back end of my kitchen cupboard (half-opened pack of barley, tin of French beans and dried onion, anyone?) and so never have the benefit of a 'free' meal – one involving no extra shopping costs that week. And spending a few minutes going through cheaper options for travel can trigger real savings. The next few chapters tackle just these kinds of issues: how to cut the cost of necessities you're not going to stop needing – food, clothes, dry-cleaning, furniture, transport – without having to scrimp.

Some of these require a fair amount of organisation. It's very often cheaper to go food shopping in specialist stores (butcher, market stalls) rather than the supermarket, but how many of us have the time to do that every week? What I do is blitz the butcher (who offers cheaper cuts – see page 137) once every two months or so and ram the spoils in a drawer of the freezer so I don't have to buy 'emergency' £5 chicken breasts smothered in cellophane from the meat aisle at the supermarket. On top of that, every few months I make a list of my usual weekly purchases on the grocery comparison site mysupermarket.com. That way, even though I don't usually buy food online, I can see if one supermarket has become cheaper for the contents of my usual trolley, or has special deals that would lessen my overall bill enough to make a trip worthwhile.

There are loads of ways you can save money in the kitchen, such as discovering the website where factory workers list the own-brand products that are nigh on identical to their pricier alternatives (see page 135), or growing your own fruit and veg. Pick and choose the ideas that fit your lifestyle, and once they become second nature you'll be saving tons each year. Don't forget about eating out, too: I visit far more restaurants nowadays than pre-recession because eateries are frankly far better value. The top ones have super-cheap lunch deals, and local restaurants and chains offer two-for-one deals that can sometimes work out cheaper than buying the ingredients yourself at home. That's perfect ausperity: making life easier for yourself with a night out that's better value than hours slaving over a stove.

Elsewhere in the home, why buy when you can borrow? Clothes, kids' gear, books, skills, tickets, bags and more can all be swapped and borrowed instead of being bought – see page 177. Oh, and I've also included a ton of info about cleaning, because after an I-can't-believe-how-much-they're-charging moment in the furniture-polish aisle of the supermarket, I've also spent the last few months learning loads of creative home-cleaning ideas. Did you know white vinegar can be used to clean, well, pretty much anything? I've also discovered that cola makes an unbelievably good toilet cleaner – whisks away any stains in about half an hour, which is kind of terrifying when you wonder what it does to your teeth. Still, see page 165 to stop shelling out hundreds on nasty cleaning chemicals each year.

Oh, and girls, if you've been thinking about cutting down on any of your beauty regime to save cash, check out the last chapter of 'Milking It'. You really don't have to. I asked top beauty experts about what they use for their own cosmetics and make-up, and was shocked at how many can be made yourself in the kitchen. I'm never throwing away an off egg again – and my hair is loving it.

Food and booze

Every time I'm in a supermarket, I mentally cut out ten per cent of my trolley and imagine chucking it in the bin. Not because of some anti-Tesco psychosis, but because that's how much the average British shopper ends up throwing away every single week. For most families, all that waste tots up to chucking more than £50 a month down the drain. So the simplest way to reduce that barcode-long number that is inevitably rung up at the supermarket checkout each week is this: make sure you use every last scrap of what you buy, and get through all those store cupboard delights you already have at home. Even those lentils you bought in a fit of healthiness nine months ago.

Cooking too much and food going off – either totally untouched, or opened but never finished – are the two main reasons shoppers explain away their pile-up of bin-food. But it won't take much organisation to cut out that waste, leaving an extra £600 in your wallet each year. Just think how much Häagen-Dazs or how many mini-breaks you could spend that on . . .

Fridge audit

The first step is a fridge audit. Sound confusing? Well, there's no need to call in a City bean-counter for this one: you can do it yourself. Starting can feel scary. When I did my first fridge audit, a jar of ready-chopped garlic was so rigidly stuck to a shelf that I had to use a fish slice and hammer (in truth, not an actual hammer, but a nearby jar of jam, which did the job excellently) to dislodge it. So yes, the first fridge audit will take time, and possibly a bit of manual dexterity, but the first step is just to methodically work through your fridge and check the 'use-by' and 'best-before' dates on all of its contents. Supermarkets have worked out cunning ways to encourage shoppers into their aisles more often, and one of them is via the confusing dates on their when-to-eat-by labels.

The truth and nothing but: food labels

The main date you need to watch out for is the use-by date: that's the one food safety experts warn is the last day on which food should be eaten. With the sole exception of eggs, best-before dates are more flexible. After the date has passed, a food's flavour or looks might start to fade, but don't be ageist: it will usually taste fine. As for 'display until' warnings, these are just for the shop assistants: you can display your food as much as you want to (and may I say, your pyramid of tins of kidney beans is looking lovely today).

So with that food labelling info in mind, you need to go through your fridge shelves and work out how and when you're going to use any perishable items nearing their death-date as soon as possible. Maybe there's a hodgepodge of weird vegetables about to go off. Don't hurl them in the bin and feel guilty, just grind them down into a soup – for a future meal via the freezer if you're not peckish now. I bought a £5 stick blender from Argos a year ago and it's cost-per-use must be down in the demi-pennies by now. Soup-making is one of the easiest and most satisfying things you can do in the kitchen. Just fry an onion, possibly a leek too if you have one hanging around, until brown, then toss in a miscellany of vegetables. (Odd bunch of root veg? Call it a winter vegetable soup. In need of a cheap meal? Chuck in half a bag of frozen peas and a handful of mint or herbs.) After a minute or two of frying, pour in boiling water and stock, then use a stick blender to whizz it up and, hey presto, your dying vegetables have been resuscitated as a meal.

Other foods I've recently brought back from the edge include some small chunks of cheese – just grate them and sprinkle on top of your soup for a really soup-er (sorry) dinner. An ageing yogurt is the basis of a really excellent smoothie, and a helluva lot cheaper than the astonishing prices cafés charge. Oh, and just tonight, a punnet of squidgy, cracking tomatoes made the base of a delicious pasta sauce for my dinner buddies.

So be imaginative during your fridge audit. And move any food that you're not going to be able to gobble soon enough into the freezer. You can't overestimate the huge array of food that's rescuable thanks to the joy of freezing. Think pints – or even part pints – of milk, large packets of chicken or fish fillets (divide them up and freeze them in individual portions, because rare is the night you'll want to demolish ten chicken breasts in one meal), and bags of sliced bread. (That way you can just take out a couple of slices when you need them, and they defrost in seconds in the toaster. It's surprisingly easy to dislodge slices when frozen – even I, with weedy arm muscles unable to remove garlic jars from fridge shelves, can do it.) Any dregs of beer or wine (OK, it's unlikely, but on the off chance . . .) should be poured into ice cube trays and frozen. Then you can drop them into future stews, fondues or casseroles and won't have to crack open a bottle of booze especially for the recipe – because we all know those half-drunk bottles don't tend to hang around long . . .

'Nobody (in our house at least) gets excited by leftovers. They sit in the fridge, glaring malevolently at me whenever I open the door. So instead I freeze leftover portions as complete individual meals, so that a meal can be produced very quickly. My son at uni thinks I'm really well organised . . . I'm not – I just hate throwing away food. I also cut cake up into portions to freeze.' – ANNE, LONDON

If you're creative, you'll find a use for everything. Some bananas on the turn will be perfect for a banana cake – the mushier the bananas, the moister the cake. Found a lemon that's more wrinkled than a British bulldog? Squeeze it hard and it will weep out some lemon juice, which you can pour into an ice cube tray if you don't need it now; it'll make a refreshing addition to a drink on a future evening. Discovered half a jar of leftover pesto or pasta sauce? Freeze it in a Tupperware box or a closable sandwich bag for later use. Even a packet of stale crisps, cereal, nuts or crackers that have gone soft and soggy can be brought back to life in the resus. room (pretend you're on *ER* or *Casualty*) of your kitchen: just bake them in the oven for a few minutes, then let them cool, and they'll harden right up again to be crisp and crunchy once more.

Elsewhere in the kitchen, that gnarled end of a loaf of bread that no one likes can be broken up into croutons for soup or breadcrumbs to top a pasta bake. Again, the breadcrumbs will happily freeze if you don't need them pronto. Or add them to mince to bulk up (and bring down the cost of) burgers or meatballs. Likewise, bits of stale cake or biscuits can be scooped into a sandwich bag and smashed up with a rolling pin into crumbs to top desserts or crumbles. And if you've made a cake that's sunk faster than *Titanic* in the centre, don't even think about throwing it away (or, more likely if you're anything like me, polishing it off solo because it's not fit for company) – just fill the middle with cream and fruit, shake out some icing sugar on top and call yourself Nigella. Or Heston or Gordon, if they are more your thing.

Any unripened fruit that you need to be ready immediately, say before you go away on holiday, can just be popped in a brown bag with a banana. Bananas are like the magic ripenator that the manufacturing world hasn't yet invented: they ensure everything is ready to eat in double-quick time. In my experience, that includes every single time I put a banana and any other fruit in my handbag. One or the other will explode. All of my handbags have darkened, hardened patches inside from where a piece of fruit met its explosive end – I never learn.

If you've anything else leftover in your fridge that you can't work out how to use or freeze before it goes off, flick through a recipe book for inspiration or check out the websites supercook.com and allrecipes.com. Just type in your list of lingering ingredients, and they will offer up thousands of ideas to find a use for leftovers.

Fridge audit over, now it's time to do exactly the same thing with your freezer (you can't store everything in a freezer forever – it's not cryogenic). Work out how long you can keep things via this informative site: fsis.usda.gov. And remember to write dates on everything that's going beyond your freezer doors from now on.

Once the freezer work is over, it's on to the store cupboards. Challenge yourself to use up things you've got. Find a way to use up those weird-looking beans that were going cheap that time and haven't yet hit your dinner plates, or that funny-sounding rice that's been lingering for a few months, which will not only provide a cheap meal (you've already laid out for the main ingredient), but give you more cupboard space too – meaning you can stock up on the best bulk deals. But more on that later.

Your first food audit will take a while. It might even morph into a cleaning spree, since unsticking that four-year-old pack of Pot Noodle or pasta from its shelf might need a bit of elbow grease (cheap cleaning: see page 165), and a freezer clear-out will inevitably lead to a defrosting bonanza. But once the first one is out the way, you'll start thinking about your food shopping differently – and end up knowing more than just your onions.

Supermarket shopping

Ah, shopping. When I was little, I used to view a trip to the supermarket as a real treat. It would mean annoying my mum as she pushed a trolley around the store trying to concentrate on finding the ingredients she needed for the week whilst I tugged at her sleeve asking, then suggesting, then eventually begging, for various chocolate treats.

Then I moved to university, and away from home, and food shopping was no longer a once-in-a-half-term treat but a weekly necessity. And it became boring. And expensive. And a chore. But as I worked out how the supermarkets were luring me in like a brainless blob, I decided to find a way to eat well, pay less and beat them at their own game. *Beat the Supermarket*: it could be a top new panel game, the opposite of *Supermarket Sweep*. Here's how to play . . .

The first rule is this: never, ever enter a supermarket without a list. These places spend millions of pounds employing retail scientists (those Mickey Mouse degree students you once mocked are having the last laugh now) to work out the very best way to wring out the maximum amount of money from your bank account every time you pass through their doors. It's no coincidence that there's a really nice bread-baking smell oozing down the aisles and it's making your tummy rumble. It's more than likely being pumped out with the sole purpose of doing just that – because people buy and spend more when they're hungry. That cheaper range of baked beans you can't find? That's because the (more expensive) items supermarkets really want you to buy are stocked at eye-level, whilst the ones on offer or just costing less require a bit of neck straining. And if you're wondering why the peas you just know were in aisle twenty-three last week have moved this week, again, it's no accident: the layout of a supermarket will often be shifted around in a bid to disorientate shoppers – in the hope that doing so will encourage you and me to visit more of the store, and buy more.

That's why the best way to combat all this confusion is the list. Before leaving the house, sit down and plan when you and/or your flatmates, family, pet dog and goldfish are eating at home over the next week or two, and when you or anyone else in the family is eating out and could save money by taking packed food. Then write down the necessary ingredients. Planning meals ahead of time means you can avoid buying anything you don't need. (A by-product of this technique is you avoid buying that family-sized pack of chocolates and might lose weight. Unless you're me, and you then go and buy an overpriced single bar of Cadbury's Dairy Milk on the way home as a 'rare treat' – in which case, buy a pack and hide them.)

If you always find yourself buying and cooking over-generous portions of meals – and that's why food ends up in the bin – then take a visit to lovefoodhatewaste.com whilst making your list. It's a brilliant site that will help you work out perfect portions for a huge range of meals, including exactly what quantities you'll need for your household. Before I logged in, I once made lasagne for two people with so many ingredients it lasted us six meals. Once I'd got over the feeling that I never, ever wanted to see pasta or white sauce again, I found this site. It's really easy to use: just enter the details of what you're cooking, including the ingredients and number of people who will be chowing down (the site works out different amounts for adults and kids), and it will tell you exactly how much to buy and cook. Mashed potatoes for six adults and three children? That's fifteen heaped tablespoons of spuds. Portions of plaice for four adults? You'll be needing 560 grams of fish. There are also dish-based quantities. But unfortunately, it doesn't have a portion planner for lasagne.

'Buy in bulk – if you know you need to buy more, then buy lots in one go. It will reduce the cost.' – SADIA, HORLEY

Use the site to help you compile your list, and just before you leave the house, list in hand, consider another easy way to avoid succumbing to temptation: shopping online. Find a voucher for free delivery – see page 18 on online shopping – and log on. You'll certainly find it's easier to stick to your list this way. Also online, you can keep tabs on the best foodie deals at the site mysupermarket.com. It's a grocery comparison website that makes it easy to add all the items you want to your virtual trolley. The site will then calculate the price of your shopping at supermarkets including Waitrose, Ocado, Sainsbury's, Tesco and Asda. It saves the list so you can see each week where would be cheaper, and you can easily tweak the list and either send the order to the supermarket you choose and order online, or print it off and visit it.

In-store money saving

Money-saving supermarket entrance tip: if you're popping into a shop with the intention of stocking up with just a few goods, take a basket, not a trolley, to avoid falling victim to I-want-to-fill-it-itus. Once you're in store, make the most of buy-one-get-one-frees and all their discount relatives – *but only if the items are on your list* or you can swap them with something that is. We've all fallen into the old 'buying-things-we-don't-need-because-they're-on-discount' trap before – but remember, that's the reason you just went through your store cupboard and wondered why you own two bags of sugar cubes that you've never opened.

So before you succumb to any off-list deal, make sure you obey the second rule: be sure you're going to use every single one of those discounted goods, and at a rate that you'll be able to do so before they go off. Four loaves of bread for £2 is great value if you're going to use them all. If three are going to end up mouldy because they don't fit in the freezer, then that's just a waste of money.

Do use deals to stock up on cheap non-perishables like tins of vegetables or toilet roll if you have space to store the extra ones or a friend to share the cost with. In fact, anyone who lives in a small household should try sharing a shopping trip with a friend now and then to capitalise on those bulk buys. Sure, going on a shopping spree with mates used to mean splurging on a new dress, not a great deal on frozen peas, but think of it as a new ausperity Britain bonding experience . . .

In the fruit and vegetables aisle, buy loose: they're cheaper than their packaged alternatives. Reuse the plastic or brown bags they come in (or pick up a few extra from the roll) to avoid having to buy a box of sandwich bags. Sounds tight, but saving £2 a month by not buying packaging adds up to £24 a year – think of it as an evening for two at the cinema. And buy products that are in season locally because they will be plentiful and therefore cheaper. In winter, that's root vegetables like turnips and carrots, and citrus fruits like lemons and oranges; in summer, it's fruit such as berries, tomatoes and grapes. If you're not sure, the price will be a strong indicator.

Ignore the adverts

Throughout the store, try trading down from a brand to a supermarket-range item or from the latter to its value-range sister. Sometimes, you'll notice a difference and may not like it – in which case, once you've finished the packet, just go back to your original choice. But most of the time, you'll find the only thing you were paying extra for was that cereal maker or tinned vegetable producer spending half the packet price on churning out a nauseating TV ad, and the food tastes the same. I once had an argued-till-we-were-red-in-the-face-and-then-I-started-crying blow up with my fiancé over Shreddies. OK, it only started on Shreddies and went on to bigger issues. But he was adamant a supermarket own-brand alternative was just as good, while I was sure Shreddies could never be replicated. Then one morning he swapped the Shreddies packet for its cheaper, 'Wholegrain Wheats', alternative without me knowing. And I didn't notice, until he pointed it out a week later, extremely smugly. In fact, he still harks back to it every time I lose an argument.

But really it's no wonder it was hard to detect, because supermarket-branded food is often made in the very same factory as its pricier alternatives. And if you're feeling snobby about it, you can always decant your value-branded food into tall Tupperwares – even the Queen pours her cereal from a Tupperware, so who's to say it's not Wholegrain Wheats she's eating too?

Visit supermarketownbrandguide.co.uk to find the best own-brands. The site hosts reviews of more than 8,000 products, revealing which are worth trading down for. The site also has an app, called 'Can I eat it', which is available to iPhone users and may be useful whilst in the supermarket. And just in case you're wondering, the Co-operative's Wholegrain Wheats version of Shreddies is rated ten out of ten, with the review 'similar quality to the leading brand, but at a cheaper price. Put a pack in the trolley.' I didn't write it.

I'll eat it, honest

Throughout your food shopping visit, make sure you're being honest with yourself. Unless your name is Nigella Lawson (in which case, hi! I love your chocolate cake recipe), you're probably not going to be able to be a smug domestic god(dess) making home-made food every day. That's why it's important to plan for those evenings when you're too knackered to cook: always stock up on a few frozen meals like pizza or a packet of ravioli. They work out cheaper than a takeaway, but are almost as easy.

If you're passing by a supermarket near closing time, it's often worth popping in and following the guy with the gun. Nope, not a sniper, but the holder of the reductions gun who wanders around the shop slapping discounts all over the place. It's always worth having a chat to them – if they're in a good mood they'll tell you what they're going to be reducing in the next aisle or two. Follow the gun for four or so items, and challenge yourself to whip up a meal with the results, *Ready Steady Cook*-style. Or capitalise on the biggest discounts, but again, obviously only if you've got a use for the products.

I've seen sandwiches for 10p, and huge tubs of cream for 3p. Pop that in the freezer or whip up some scones. (Possibly the easiest-ever thing to bake: mix together 225g self-raising flower, 55g butter, 25g caster sugar, 150ml milk and a pinch of salt. Roll the mixture out on a board to about 2cm high, use a biscuit-cutter to form scones, brush the top with a beaten egg, then bake for 12–15 minutes – and you've found a very cheap way to entertain friends for tea.)

Go local

It's a good idea to explore other shops in your neighbourhood too. Supermarkets are brilliant for convenience, but don't forget you can get better deals, and build up loyalty discounts, by shopping at local markets (many do big bowls of various fruits for £1) and shops. Last week, my local butcher sold five pounds of chicken fillets for £14. Buying the same amount in Tesco would have cost £24. To find a butcher in your local area, visit findabutcher.co.uk. And ask that butcher to help you learn to love cheap cuts of meat. Cuts like the unfashionable but still tasty lamb shoulder are great for stews or curries. Another bargain cut is beef skirt. It's beloved by the French (who call it the *onglet*), but traditionally ignored here because, one butcher told me, 'it tastes very beefy'. But isn't that what you want from beef? Also try meat portions such as a duck leg rather than breast, pork or ox cheeks, ham hocks and chicken livers. For beef, cheaper cuts like the breast, shins and flank make great stews and casseroles.

'I try to buy fruit and vegetables from greengrocers, and go little and often, which means I don't waste so much. I enjoy cooking, never buy ready-made food and make my own soups – they taste better and are cheaper.' – JILL, MANCHESTER

Elsewhere, bargain stores like Aldi and LIDL can be cheaper for bulk buys like pasta, rice or frozen foods. You have to be flexible about meal plans, though. The last time I checked, LIDL had two huge stone-baked frozen pizzas for £2.50 and a 7.5kg pack of baking potatoes for £1.99. If you've got a big family – or a lot of home storage – you might want to consider joining a cash and carry store like Costco (costco.co.uk), which has twenty-two warehouses in the UK. There is a £30 annual membership fee, but fans say they save more than that by bulk-buying. Other similar chains include Booker (booker.co.uk) and Makro (makro. co.uk). Don't overlook pound shops either. Branded items like pasta, rice and baking products are much cheaper. But be careful to stay alert: make sure none of the products have expired – or if they have, that it's not a problem (see page 125) – and don't be blind to prices: often not every item in a pound store actually costs a pound.

Again, since none of us is superman with a zillion hours to use up in a week and a cape to fly around with, remember you can easily mix up these trips to the butcher, baker, candlestick maker and pound shop, popping in occasionally to stock up – and save money.

Poun' for a box

Make the most of market stalls that sell food that is surplus or close to the end of its shelf life for low prices. I've snapped up a box of a hundred packets of Smarties for a couple of quid – providing an excellent midday snack for months and making me very popular with colleagues – just because they only had a month left on their use-by date.

Online shops offer similar deals for those who don't have a suitable market nearby. Approvedfood.co.uk, for example, claims to help shoppers save an average sixty to eighty per cent on their weekly shop with deals like packets of Loyd Grossman pasta sauce for 20p, twenty-eight packets of Hula Hoops for £1.60, plus offers on toiletries, drinks and gifts.

Whilst you're online, other bargain-providing foodie web sites on my favourites list include fixtureferrets.co.uk, which lists the best deals in supermarkets, including the buy-one-get-one-frees which are worth stocking up on. And anyone who likes a glass of red or white of an evening can cut the cost of their tipple by checking out quaffersoffers. co.uk: it lists the best wine prices at both supermarkets and individual stores.

Keep hotukdeals.com on whatever the online equivalent of speed dial is, too. I check in every day, as the very simply-laid out website is a forum where members post the top offers currently available online – and since many of the best offers are as a result of someone's fat finger, the deals are often pulled from sale as little as a few hours or even minutes after going up. The more popular a deal, the closer it goes to the top of the website, so you don't have to look far for a bargain. The site was recently spreading the news of a glitch at the tills in Tesco which meant shoppers could buy Terry's Chocolate Oranges for 29p, rather than the usual £2.75. One chocoholic bought nearly 200 chocolate oranges for £56. Saving £472 in sterling, but perhaps putting on rather more than that in pounds of another sort . . .

DIY food

Let's step away from the computer again to focus on an old-school way to save serious cash in the kitchen: going DIY, or make what you could buy. Whatever your current regime, add some more home-made elements to it and you'll save money. Eat takeouts five times a week? Switch some of them to an easy home-made pasta sauce and pasta. To make a pasta bake for four: fry an onion until light brown, add a handful of chopped mushrooms, courgettes, peppers or any of your favourite veg, then a whole tin of chopped tomatoes and a teaspoon of mixed herbs or window-sill basil (see below). Add a twist of salt and pepper, squeeze in a dollop of tomato purée or ketchup if you need a sweetener; bring the pasta to the boil in another pan, drain and mix the two together in an oven dish. Sprinkle a generous portion of any cheese on top, add a handful of breadcrumbs if you've got some handy, bake for twenty minutes and enjoy. If there's only one or two of you, for the same effort you can freeze half for another night's dinner, or eat it for the next day's lunch.

If you already cook a lot but usually use ready-made ingredients like bought stock, you can make your own to save extra pennies. Home-made stocks and sauces are always cheaper than bought ones and are seriously easy. Next time you have a roast chicken, for example, and have already stripped down the carcass for a risotto, just drop the bones into a large saucepan and fill it up with boiling water and a dash of salt, pepper and herbs. Leave it to boil, then simmer, and skim off the fat with a spoon. Ta da! You have a portion of stock ready to be used or frozen for a future date.

Having a well-stocked freezer is an easy food money-saver, and the experts at voucher site save.co.uk say it's a growing trend. 'After a long day, the last thing we want to do is plan a healthy and tasty meal, hit the grocery store to pick up ingredients, spend twenty minutes prepping and then thiry minutes cooking. So freezer cooking is growing in popularity. Spend one day putting together several meals to freeze for future use. Then for just one day of work, you'll save time and money and have pre-made meals to enjoy whenever you have time. All you have to do is take a meal out in the morning to defrost and pop it in the oven when you get home. Knowing that you're fully stocked means no more last-minute trips through the drive-through or fast food cheeseburgers. And when you buy ingredients in bulk, you can stock up on sale items and save money.'

Eating out

Austerity may mean stopping eating out but ausperity doesn't. In fact, Britain's economic doldrums have actually forced a host of eateries to lower their prices, and with vouchers too – and staying away from the drinks menu – it can be cheaper to eat out than in. Even special occasion dinners cost less now the country's poshest restaurants have started to feel the impact of Britons' emptier wallets. So when you want to go out to eat as a treat, make the most of the special deals they're putting on to try to lure customers.

If you're keen to go somewhere specific, either phone the restaurant to ask about special deals or Google its name plus 'voucher'. But if you're not picky, check out the list of (mostly chain) eateries offering discounts at vouchercode. co.uk or moneysavingexpert.com. Smartphone users should download an app like Vouchercloud, which is free and uses a phone's GPS system to flag up discounts at restaurants near your location. That means even when you're out and about and peckish you can find a half-price meal. And don't forget to scour group buying sites like Groupon, Wowcher and LivingSocial, (see page 24) which often include meal deals in their daily offers.

In fact, restaurants are one of the major ways in which you can turn the economic downturn to your advantage. Some of the country's best eateries, the ones that are always booked up and stuffed full of celebrities, have amazing deals on at the moment – particularly for lunch. A group of friends and I have started to visit one of the upmarket restaurants in the former Conran Group (now owned by D&D London) as a regular treat. Where once their meals plus a glass of wine would be way out of our budget at £50 a head or more, now they regularly offer special, fixed-price meals to diners who book in advance and eat at particular times – normally midweek, lunchtime or Sunday nights. It means we can eat like kings but pay like paupers, and skip the washing-up too. A recent meal deal we enjoyed was a £10 three-course lunch with a glass of wine at the Thames-side Cantina del Ponte – which would normally cost something north of £50. Meanwhile, I hear good things about the three-course lunch available at the moment for £30 at Gordon Ramsay's restaurant at London's Claridge's Hotel. It's available every day, including over the weekend, and I can't wait to visit. Now that's ausperity.

For discounts at local restaurants, especially those which aren't part of a national chain, check out toptable.co.uk, where diners can search by area for eateries ranging from Michelin-starred restaurants to cafés. The site has deals (such as fifty per cent off, or £15 for three courses) at restaurants around the country, and every booking adds points to users' accounts. Once you reach a certain number of points, you can book a free meal. Or for last-minute bookings, another restaurant reservation site, 5pm.co.uk, is worth a visit.

If there's a pricey restaurant you're particularly keen on visiting, it's worth attempting some last-minute, light bargaining. On quiet midweek evenings, for example, especially if the weather's rubbish, it's worth phoning to see if the manager will allow you to order off a lunchtime deal for dinner.

Anyone who regularly eats out should work out whether it could be worth signing up to a discount scheme like the Gourmet Society (which offers up to fifty per cent off more than 5,000 restaurants for £45 a year) or Taste London (for £70 a year, card holders receive fifty per cent off meals at 5,500 restaurants). In both cases, there are free trials available, so sign up to those first to see if you would get your money's worth. Also, both cards have time restrictions in place for a lot of deals, so it's worth investigating those, plus how many restaurants near your home are part of the schemes, before signing up.

Wherever you end up, before ordering, take note of the restaurant bill-cutting tips from save.co.uk's users (they might help cut waistlines too). 'Skip the starter altogether or make a salad at home before you go out – you will save money and avoid overindulging. As soon as your main arrives, request a takeaway box and put half your meal in it. You'll be glad you did – not only do you save a ton of calories but you also get an extra meal out of it. Or share a main course: many restaurants give you astronomical portions so even if you share, you'll still have plenty to eat.

'And be loyal. If a restaurant has a loyalty programme, join it and you'll earn points every time you go. Even if a restaurant you love doesn't have a loyalty programme, you'll quickly become a familiar face. Regulars tend to get special treatment in the form of discounts and free stuff.'

Don't do all that work saving money on the food just to send the bill into the stratosphere with drink. Unless you're a wine buff or celebrating a special occasion, you should probably stick to the house red or white for the sake of affordability. And watch out for waiters trying to up-sell on water, too. They'll often use phrases such as 'still or sparkling?' or 'everyone having water?' to lure you in. But tap water is free, so just firmly respond that 'tap water will be fine, thanks'. Ask for a slice of lemon to go with it and it'll taste just as good as the £4 bottle they were about to serve you.

For a last bit of old-school money-saving in restaurants, don't forget about bring-your-own-booze joints. There are far more around now than at the start of the recession, and you can find a list of BYOB restaurants, including details of corkage fees, at wine-pages.com.

The sandwich box

In my years of writing about money-saving for various newspapers, there was one tip that readers kept sending in that I was happy to pass on but terrible at sticking to myself: packed lunches. People would email in and tell me they were saving £20 a week just by making their sarnies themselves rather than picking up a wrap at Pret or a pasty at Greggs. But my morning routine only includes twenty minutes from alarm unkindly shrieking me awake to leaving the house. I didn't want to wake up any earlier, *and* I had bad memories of the ropey sandwiches I'd make myself every day at secondary school (bread, sandwich spread, bread – gross). So shop-bought sandwiches were my one luxury.

But eventually, buying the same few sandwiches every week stopped feeling like a treat and I realised that, even though I'd only buy one roll and bring a banana, bar of chocolate or something else from home, that single sandwich was costing more than £15 a week. The maths soon becomes scary: £60 a month, more than £700 a year. I realised that if I tried out a DIY lunch, I could save enough for a holiday. Or several blow-out lunches in the best restaurants in the world. So I did.

'Wash out polythene bags to reuse them.' – MARJORIE, NOTTINGHAM

What I learnt is this: making your own lunch doesn't have to be boring. We think of home-made sandwiches as a bit ropey because we put much less effort into them than dinner. But just adding a few sprigs of lettuce, plus cucumber and maybe some pickle or relish to a hunk of cheese and a few slices of your favourite bread makes a top snack. Be a bit imaginative and your DIY sandwich can easily work out nicer than its shop-bought alternatives. If your work has a kitchen, chuck some leftovers from dinner into a Tupperware and microwave it at lunchtime – it's supposed to be healthier to eat a big meal in the daytime than in the evening anyway.

If you're really time-poor in the mornings, think about freezing a batch of sarnies ahead of time. Try using pita bread or tortilla wraps – they freeze better with ingredients – and slap on some butter, then peanut butter, or tuna-mayo and grated carrots. Take the sandwiches out of the freezer in the morning, and they'll defrost by lunchtime. Eat within two hours of defrosting.

And whilst we're on the topic of make-it-and-take-it . . . Coffee: a word, please. That little luxury of a Starbucks a day might seem like it only costs a few quid. But add up those skinny lattes and the total bill will quickly add up to £15 a week – or £780 a year. If you're a fan of posh coffee, it will work out cheaper to buy a coffee-making machine. Otherwise, make yourself a thermos in the morning and treat yourself to a café drink once a week.

Grow your own

Few of us have the time, space, know-how or, well, the voice that would enable us to become the next Alan Titchmarsh. But who cares about his millions and book deals and TV shows when – with just one windowsill – you can find enough room to grow a couple of plants or vegetables and be almost the same as Mr T that way? A fence or set of railings – they're great to hang tubs off – or even the tiniest patches of garden can provide plentiful free salad crops for months. Lettuce is an easy starter: a loose-leaf variety like bijou, lollo rosso or salad bowl will be ready to eat as early as six weeks after sowing – just pick off individual leaves and more will grow. Herbs are great for kitchen windowsills: mine is chock-a-block with basil, mint and parsley plants that can be snapped up from a local garden centre for about £1 – about the cost of two portions of fresh leaves from a supermarket. Mine are growing happily in the plastic tubs they came in, sitting in an old saucer and providing a plentiful supply of herbs.

Other easy things to grow indoors include beansprouts: just buy some mung bean seeds, chuck a generous handful into the bottom of a washed-out jar or pot and cover with cold water. Leave them overnight, then drain them and repeat the process. They will start to sprout after just a couple of days. Keep rinsing and draining them daily, and eat them after about five days. If you've got enough room for some pots – or planting – outside, carrots, garlic and potatoes are all easy. I found a book called *How to Grow Your Food – A Guide for Complete Beginners* by Jon Clift and Amanda Cuthbert (Green Books, £5.99), a very useful, idiot-proof source of advice on planting all sorts of fruit, veg and herbs. And if all goes well and you find yourself ready to graduate from beginners' level, then consider an allotment. They've moved on a lot since Arthur Fowler's day in *EastEnders*, to the extent that many have a waiting list. But they're a brilliant way to grow your own food – including veg like potatoes, carrots, beans and more – plus flowers which can make cheap 'thank you' presents. Find out more from the National Society of Allotment and Leisure Gardeners Limited – nsalg.org.uk.

For parents, there's another bonus: kids are always much happier to eat the lettuce they watered and watched sprout than a supermarket-bought one that just looks 'green and gross and nasty'. They'll also love to forage for free food – who wouldn't? There's no better feeling than picking fruit from an autumn field or apples from a neighbour's garden, with their consent, and whipping them into an apple pie. And don't overlook the potential for blackberries (turn them into jam or crumbles, add to fruit salad), sloes (bitter round fruits that need to be cooked and can be turned into jam, jelly or sloe gin), or roadside damsons and gooseberries (easily made into a delicious dessert).

Is it legal? Well, you can't just march on to Farmer Giles's land and pick 1,000 apples, but the Theft Act 1968, for England and Wales, states: 'A person who picks mushrooms growing wild on any land, or who picks flowers, fruit or foliage from a plant growing wild on any land, does not steal what he picks, unless he does it for reward or for sale or other commercial purpose.' So if it's for your lunch, you're fine, but if it's for your jam-making factory, well, not so much.

Clothes SOS

The shopping tips a few chapters back will help you save a fortune on your clothes, but don't forget that even when a new skirt or T-shirt does cost a fiver from Primark, it will often work out better value to make do and mend. Yup, it's time to listen to the stuff your mother used to say. Those £40 jeans which have developed a rip on the knee aren't necessarily ripe for the knacker's yard: couldn't you sew a patch on and wear them for another year or more? The jeans will probably still last longer than a super-cheap replacement.

There's really no need to dump pricey clothes (that you still like – and even if you don't, read on . . .) if they just need a new button put on or zip applied. Although some things are impossible to do yourself unless you've surgeon-worthy sewing skills, hems are easily sewn up or let down on kids' clothing and little tears can be sewn up to resuscitate ripped clothes or furnishings. If you are keen to boost your mending skills, ask a friend or relative – usually those from older generations are most practised – or see if a haberdashery or other shop advertises courses. Some branches of the department store John Lewis run free knitting and sewing lessons, and in my experience the staff are usually happy to help – in the past, I've turned up with a half-knitted jumper and they were pleased to help me work out what to do next. There are also thousands of online resources such as sewing.org. They'll help you turn old jeans into denim shorts or skirts, dresses into T-shirts, jackets into waistcoats, etc.

For trickier tasks, seek out a local seamstress or tailor who will help you to fix or adapt clothes to give them a new lease of life. It's usually worth looking for someone working independently rather than within a department store or dry-cleaner, where the fees will be higher. A lady living near me does sewing work like taking in dresses and shortening trousers (a requisite for every purchase when you're five foot nothing like me) for less than a tenner. Ask around: recommendation is key – you don't want your favourite dress butchered by a dodgy sewer.

Meanwhile, remember when buying new clothes and shoes that looking after them will prolong their life. Don't fall for the sales tricks when you're buying new shoes and the assistant offers you a suede protection spray for 'only £10', but do be aware you can pick these up for £2 from local shoe repair shops, supermarkets or online. And they are worth using, especially on expensive boots like Uggs – which, and I speak from experience, go brown, weather-beaten and mottled very quickly without it.

Stuff shoes with balls of newspaper to maintain their shape when you're not wearing them – particularly if they'll be out of use for a while, like heels that you only wear for black-tie events or winter boots during summer. Hand wash clothes that demand it, and be savvy about washing labels. If one demands 'dry-clean' instead of 'dry-clean only', you may be able to get away with hand-washing the item, although for precious clothes or very delicate items you may not want to risk it. Alternatively consider using a cleaning 'sheet' which is added to the tumble drier and claims to clean delicates in a, well, delicate way.

As for clothes you can no longer stand, or the leftovers from a wardrobe clear-out that you no longer like, or which don't fit, or which you cannot understand why you ever allowed to cross the threshold of your home, you might be able to raise some cash selling them on eBay, or to a local second-hand clothing shop. Before doing so, think about whether a small, cheap alteration might change your opinion. Letting trousers out, switching buttons, adding a lace or velvet trimming or brooch or corsage, and dyeing shoes (you can buy kits yourself or go to a bridal/ bridesmaid shoe retailer – they'll advise you whether it's possible) can all transform a dull outfit or accessory into one that's exactly what you were thinking about going shopping for . . .

Home

Take a look at the British businesses that are doing well at the moment, and it becomes pretty obvious what we're all doing in our spare time. Takeaway pizza chains are posting record sales; supermarkets are tripping over themselves to offer dine-in meal deals, online e-tailers are booming . . . basically, nights in (specifically, on the sofa) are the new nights out. Now of course there are tons of ways to make going out more affordable – for tips, read pages 28–39 and you'll be running out of the house to follow them up – but since we are spending more time staying in, we're starting to notice stuff. Like the fact that – in my house anyway – a spring has not quite physically protruded from the sofa material, but lodges itself uncomfortably in any bum that happens to plonk itself on it. And the way that the oven, which was bought back in the days when prawn cocktail was *the* dinner party starter, now takes twice the recipe-recommended amount of time to bake a cake.

Just like everything else, there are three ways to pimp out your home: spend a bomb on doing so, carry out a botched job or cut corners without damaging the paintwork – that is, turn a pad into a palace without shelling out thousands. This chapter is all about how to do so – and there's a dose of old-school cleaning tips, too, that show that a sparkling-clean house doesn't need to rely on shopping sprees for trolleys full of Mr Muscle and his colleagues.

New furniture

Instead of immediately heading out to the shops, try swapping or blagging first. Most homes have furniture that the owner once bought but now hates, or has no need for. A few months ago, I had two perfect-condition Ikea bookshelves that didn't fit in my new flat hanging around, so when a friend came around and saw them, she offered to swap them for a massive beanbag she no longer wanted. She repainted the bookshelves to match her lounge, I chucked the beanbag cover in the wash and it came out sparkling; we both have new furnishings without paying a penny – and, possibly even better, without having to spend half a weekend in Ikea.

Nobody likes throwing things out, so ask friends and family if they have any unwanted furniture hanging around before buying. It's also worth keeping a beady eye on the goods coming up on your local freecycle (uk.freecycle. org) site. It might be just what you want, or it might be hideous, but possible to transform with a lick of paint or remodelling. Once you've snaffled the goods, there are lots of advice sites on the internet – just search for your piece of furniture and desired transformation on Google or YouTube.

Oh, and don't forget just how much a bit of DIY can save you. Moving house – or having kids, animals and other destructive forces living with you all the time – can take its toll. Bookshelves collapse, floors are scratched, crucial parts are lost . . . But your immediate response shouldn't be to head out to buy a replacement – just try to fix them. A shopping spree to pick up tools, nails, glue and other fixers will cost far less than a replacement, and be more satisfying too. Local colleges host household maintenance courses, whilst libraries offer how-to books, and online videos may also offer help. You can also save money whilst getting something new(ish) by doing some DIY refurbishment work. It's not difficult to re-cover a chair if you've got a sewing machine or even a hefty staple gun. Tables, cabinets and cupboard doors can be altered or stripped down and refinished. Sofas are trickier, but even then it'll be cheaper to pay for expert reupholstering than buying a new one. It's an easy way to get unique pieces of furniture for far less than it would cost to buy new.

One last piece of advice before we visit the best-value stores: sometimes it's much cheaper to spend more but buy once. Because some things are worth investing in. A flat-pack bed, for example, may not survive many house moves intact, whilst a good hand-made wooden bed frame will probably live longer than you. So know what you're buying. Some furniture retailers will cover MDF-style boarding in veneer and ramp up the price. Shop around, and look all over the furniture – for a bed, for example, look underneath it, at the inside of any storage drawers, and behind the headboard for clues as to the quality of the build. In the long run, it's better to spend, say, £500 on a great bed that lasts over a decade than £200 on one that lasts a few years, then demands replacement. That's also true for mattresses: cheap ones don't last very long, so if you can afford it, it's worth going for a pricier option that comes with a long guarantee.

Now, on to the shopping. The best way to buy furniture, says Alison Cork, of money-saving homes site alisonathome. co.uk, is to 'turn the calendar upside down'. She explains:

'Buy your garden furniture in winter and your fireplaces in the summer – these are tougher months for seasonal products so clearance sales are often the only way to get punters through the doors. Aside from the key sales periods of Boxing Day and bank holidays, it's worth finding out launch dates for new spring, summer, autumn and winter collections – because you can bet that a clearance will be just around the corner.'

It's also worth veering off-piste. The likes of Ikea and Argos offer bargain-bucket furniture, but check out the furniture on offer in out-of-town warehouses and industrial estates too. Trade Secret, for example, is an outlet furniture warehouse in Oxford that sells cancelled orders and over-runs from British brands like John Lewis and House of Fraser across its 20,000-square-foot store (trade-secret.co.uk). And watch out for sales too: find listings of the latest home retailers' clearance deals at homesandbargains.co.uk/sales-and-vouchers.

It's a good idea to find a local builder and ask them about sourcing the best quality products and raw materials at the lowest-possible prices, Cork adds. And if you can't afford it, make it yourself. If you're buying designer solid wood furniture, send a link or picture of what you want to a local carpenter. He or she will probably be able to match it for design and quality at a fraction of the price.

Try haggling. Furniture stores are having it really tough at the moment – just how tough is made clear by high-profile business failures like Habitat, but it's true too amongst small operators – and that means they are willing to chuck in freebies and cut prices to secure a deal. 'When haggling, ask to speak to the manager, who will always be in the position to give you the best price,' says Cork.

'Also, sell them the story – the more they like you, the more they'll be inclined to offer a better price. Offer to pay cash for a discount and put the money in their hand to close the sale – a bird in the hand and all that. Look through off-cuts and see if there's anything going spare that you can take off their hands.'

Be wary of those furniture payment plans that scream at you when you switch on the TV or open a newspaper. One of my friends spent longer paying off her sofa than sitting on it after signing up for a dodgy deal. Most offer a very generous-sounding interest-free payment period but, after that, force buyers to pay expensive rates. So only sign up if you know you'll be able to pay off the balance before the end of the zero per cent interest deal, or have a back-up plan in place and watch out for penalties for early repayment. In general, it's often cheaper in the long-run to buy using an interest-free credit card (see page 227).

Try second-hand furniture stores, including those run by charities: the Red Cross, for example, sells everything from sofas to appliances like washing machines at its charity shops, including dedicated furniture and electrical charity shops. Unlike a private purchase, you have the peace of mind of knowing that all furniture and electrical items sold comply with current health and safety standards. Oxfam also has dedicated furniture stores around the country, as does the Salvation Army and Emmaus (emmaus.org. uk/find), which has 'upcycled' furniture where people who have been homeless and unemployed get to work transforming pieces. If you can't get to its shops, the charity also sells its goods via eBay. Charity furniture shops sell everything from massive wardrobes to crockery and lamps. The theory goes that the closer the shop to the nicest part of town, the better the stock. Most stores offer a (paid-for) delivery service, or if not will be able to recommend a local delivery service or taxi company, or check out shiply.com (see page 188) if it's a long distance from your home.

Look out for local council-run upcycling schemes too. Barnet council in north London, for example, has a scheme which aims to provide good-quality furniture at prices to suit all budgets, prevent that furniture from being fly-tipped or going to landfill, and provide job opportunities and volunteering placements for residents including the long-term unemployed and those with disabilities. The furniture has two-tiered pricing, depending on buyers' level of household income – but there are other versions around the country, so ask your council to find out more.

New buys

Here are the best-value furniture shopping destinations from around the UK and the web, according to Cork at alisonathome.co.uk: 'What some people might not know is that major high street furniture brands make much of their furniture to order, so cancelled orders or returns are offloaded to out-of-town warehouses. These warehouses aren't allowed to shout too loudly, but current season, branded furniture is all at least fifty per cent off what you'd normally pay. Examples include Trade Secret, plus Home Brands (homebrands.co.uk) and London Warehouse (londonwarehouse.co.uk).

'For designer-quality furniture at high street prices, check out made.com which manages stock levels by running production against orders placed during a given period.

It links up manufacturers across the Far East, Europe and elsewhere with buyers, listing details of new products and then placing an exact order with the maker, thus cutting out warehouse costs and saving you money. You'll wait a little longer for your furniture to arrive, but that blow is softened by what it claims is a saving of some seventy per cent on similar quality elsewhere. For replicas of designer classics like Van de Rohe, Eames and Knoll at prices that make the real thing blush, try Milan Direct (milandirect.co.uk).'

Fabrics and wallpaper

Discounted fabrics and wallpapers are available online, but understandably the manufacturers are very stringent on how their brand is used in marketing. Top Designer (top-designer.co.uk) and Kingdom Interiors (kingdominteriors.co.uk) both stock most of the big names in the world of wallpaper at better prices than you'll pay in the local design studio. For designer curtains, try Curtain Factory Outlet (curtainfactoryoutlet.co.uk) and Loose Ends Fabrics (looseendsfabrics.co.uk).

Bathrooms

When it comes to bathrooms, a quick Google search will yield thousands of retailers working hard to secure your custom. Some of the best discounts can be found at Better Bathrooms (betterbathrooms.com), Screwfix (screwfix.com) and Heat and Plumb (heatandplumb.com), where regular sales and clearances keep prices keen. Though not available to buy online, Rotherhithe-based F.E.E.T International offers jaw-dropping value for money across a range of designer baths, shower units and tiles (feet-international.co.uk). Expect to save as much as eighty per cent on equivalent quality and design.

Kitchens

For contemporary kitchens, Kitchen Discount Centre (kdcuk.co.uk) offers imported German, high-gloss kitchens at up to thirty per cent less than you'd expect to pay on the high street. If you're looking for more traditional kitchens, Stratford-based Paragon Furniture (paragonfuniture.co.uk) offers bespoke, solid wood carpentry in a wide range of styles and woods at decent prices.

If you're looking for a kitchen worktop and it has to be granite, look no further than Granite and Marble (greekmarbles.com) where a range of granites and marbles are available at thirty to fifty per cent less than you'd pay elsewhere, with templating and installation available too. If you're looking to give your kitchen a quick update, try replacing door handles rather than the doors. Designer door handles and hinges can be picked up for up to fifty per cent less than the high street at online retailer Handle World (handleworld.co.uk).

Cushions and accessories

Cushions and accessories can be picked up online at very affordable prices if you know where to look. Cushions online (cushionsonline.co.uk) and Cushion Couture (cushioncouture.co.uk) specialise in soft furnishings and nothing else to offer exclusive designs at prices that you'll struggle to match in the department stores.

For decorative accessories, you'll struggle to beat the range on offer at Dunelm Mill (dunelm-mill.co.uk) and Matalan (matalan.co.uk) for quality and sheer value for money. For household staples, Wilkinson's (wilkinsonplus.co.uk) is also well worth a look.

Table and glassware

Out-of-town designer outlets such as McArthur Glen (mcarthurglen.com – with stores across the UK and Europe) will often play host to leading brands like Le Creuset, Oneida and Denby, as well as sales branches of high street retailers such as Next Home and Marks & Spencer. (For more outlets, see page 18.) Alternatively, most brands will have a factory shop – a quick root around the brand's website will often point you in the direction of clearance lines and slight seconds at up to fifty per cent less than you'd normally pay. Amongst the best is the Villeroy and Boch Factory Shop, Wandsworth, where uber-contemporary tableware can be picked up at a fraction of the in-store price. M&S has also just launched its outlet online (marksandspencer.com/outlet).

If you're thinking about replacing a dinner service, cutlery set or set of glasses due to a couple of missing or broken pieces, contact chinapresentations.net, lostpottery.co.uk or Chinasearch (chinasearch.co.uk) before you head to the charity shop. It stocks over a million pieces of crockery, glassware and cutlery from all the top brands including

Dartington, Alessi, Royal Worcester and Wedgwood lines that have been discontinued, so customers can top up on their tea sets rather than buy new.

Décor

For cheap wall decorations, buy bargain frames from Ikea, Wilkinson, pound shops or charity shops and fill them with arty photos, postcards, prints or wallpaper samples. Group deal sites (as set out on page 26) often run deals on photo canvases which easily turn family photos or particularly good pictures into wall artwork. A decent photo of bobbing sailing boats that I snapped on the south coast a few years ago is now stretched on a canvas as the main art in my lounge for a grand total of a tenner. Cheap fabric – try local ethnic stores – is great for covering up old sofas as a throw. Refurbish old cupboards, tables and other furniture with paint – ask for a small sample pot or buy a tester pot for small areas to save money.

Posh carpet shops sell samples of most of their designs so you can sometimes buy fairly large pieces of carpet, which can be used as lovely small rugs for a far lower price. And box clutter away in wicker baskets – I've bought ten for £10 from a local hardware store.

Building work

With less money in our pocket and not many houses hitting the property market, thousands more Britons are boosting the size of existing homes rather than moving. Sometimes this will just involve a bit of DIY, or you may need to hire a builder – or even just clearing out clutter can improve your home without spending much. 'An untidy and dirty house can really bring you down,' says Nico Springman, who, as head of interior decoration at specialist academy Inchbald School of Design, should know. 'Get rid of anything that is damaged beyond repair or has been unused for years,' he adds. 'Exceptions for items of huge sentimental value might be allowed – but get a friend to help as it concentrates the mind and an objective opinion can be useful. Then, when you buy a new piece of furniture, get rid of an old piece – sell it if you can. And do the same with clothing, crockery, toys etc.'

'Get many more years out of your PVC-U windows – members of the industry body Network VEKA report that when these windows fail before their time is up, well over half can be blamed on jammed and seized mechanisms. So instead of replacing the windows, you may only need to put a spot of oil – the liquid type, not that spray stuff – on all hinges and joints as part of your spring cleaning regime. It's that simple and only takes me a couple of minutes.'
– CHRIS, LONDON

Before you start donning the overalls and spending a weekend painting, check whether you actually need to. 'Use sugar soap – non-foaming cleaner, because it doesn't leave residue on the walls – to wash down ceilings, walls and woodwork,' says Springman. 'Then decide if a new coat of paint is required. Interiors will need painting every seven years or so, while exteriors might need it every five years – although if you live by the sea, every three years might be better.'

If you do go in for painting and want to boost your property's value, 'pale, cool colours tend to recede, so if the room feels small and it's painted a dark red, it might be time to paint it a pale violet, blue, green or grey,' says Springman. 'However, small rooms that face north or east will always seem dull, dark or grey, so it might be better to paint or paper them in a warm, darker colour like terracotta, or flame red. Go for drama and impact in such rooms, use similar colours for curtains, covers, shelves etc., and provide a contrast with the floor and the works of art on the walls or shelves. In a small room, move attention to the perimeter of the walls: banish the coffee table, the central area rug and even the central light fitting, and replace them with side tables beside sofas and chairs, with lamps on. These can be lamps with shades or directional reading lamps. Try to aim some light at the wall to get a glow off it and make it recede too.'

Other ways to make your home look expensive without great expense include buying lamp tables from a local junk shop and refreshing them with paint or varnish. Says Springman: 'New handles can make all the difference. Also, use pictures of landscapes to draw you outside the perimeter of your room. Photographs and posters, prints, paintings all help. Try larger ones than you think you need, or groups to create views and trick the eye. Or artists can try painting a *trompe l'oeil* mural to give the impression they are sitting in a different location.'

If you do need to call in the (dreaded) builders, this is an area where you shouldn't scrimp: a quote that's considerably cheaper than others is likely to come from a cowboy builder doing dodgy work that will cost much more to fix than getting the work done by a reputable provider in the first place would have done. To avoid getting ripped off, it's crucial to:

- Ask for recommendations from friends, family and neighbours. Or failing that, check out ratings on sites like ratedpeople.com and myhammer.co.uk. Always request references; some builders will be able to ask past clients if you can pay a visit to actually see their work, if it's a large-scale project similar to what you're planning.

- Call in at least three detailed quotes before starting work, and make sure they really are detailed, including exactly what work will be carried out; whether raw materials are included and, if not, what the extra costs will be; VAT; the specific dates for when the work will be started and finished; a schedule of when payments should be made, and any deposits required and paid beforehand. Never pay the entire bill before the work begins – the final payment should only be made when you're satisfied the job has been finished to the original, contracted specification. If any of the quotes are way out of the range of the others, find out why.

- Sometimes builders will offer a cheaper price if you pay with cash. This is not only illegal, but could be a sign of a disreputable tradesman. Avoid.

- If credit card payments are permitted (this is fairly rare amongst builders), opt for this because it will give you more cover if any of the work doesn't go according to plan.

Cleaning

Next time you're in the cleaning aisle of the supermarket, gazing at the gazillion brightly coloured bottles of gunk promising to wipe 150 years of grime off your oven in one spritz, or eviscerate the toilet bowl just by looking at it, think twice before purchasing. Remember your grandma's house? Wasn't it sparkling clean – in truth, probably better than your own – and all without the use of a dozen different potions? It's still possible, and possible with little more than a bottle of distilled white vinegar. There's a website, imaginatively named vinegartips.com, which lists 1,001 ways to use vinegar as a cleaning product in your home. Vinegar is acidic enough to murder most bacteria, mould and germs – and it's cheap and green too. And some might say 1,001 is still playing it down. One part vinegar and one part water will give a good clean to any glass, mirror, tiled floor or work surface. Cleaning dirty windows with that vinegar solution and old newspaper helps them sparkle, according to Springman, of Inchbald School of Design. 'Check a small, unobtrusive, area before you tackle something,' he adds. 'Vinegar works on chrome, porcelain, glass, etc., but be cautious with an enamelled or fibreglass bath, or plastic items, and do not scrub too hard.'

Vinegar will clean all counter tops (use a cloth soaked in undiluted, white distilled vinegar) and clear drains (one cup baking soda, one cup hot, white distilled vinegar, let it sit for five minutes, then run hot water down the drain). It will also clean the microwave. (Put half a cup of vinegar and half a cup of water in a microwave-safe bowl. Bring it to a rolling boil inside the microwave. Baked-on food will be loosened, and odours disappear, report vinegartips. com, and I can confirm it! Then wipe clean.) Seriously, there really are 998 further uses of vinegar for cleaning on the vinegartips.com site – and whilst I haven't yet done them all, the dozens I've tried have all been astonishingly effective. Other suggested uses involve pets, cars, laundry and the garden. You might never buy any other cleaning product again. But if you want a bit more variety, here are some old-school cleaning methods . . .

Two parts lemon juice and one part olive oil in a recycled spray bottle will polish up wood and other furniture nicely (and that's a pledge). Leave cheap supermarket own-brand cola bubbling in your loo to clean the toilet bowl. Or use up flat Coke that you don't want to drink any more – you'll be amazed how well it works. Dissolved denture tablets – the cheap own-brand ones work fine – are great at getting rid of tea stains in mugs and water marks in vases.

'With old, but not antique furniture, a little bit of tomato ketchup on the brass handles works a treat,' says Springman, speaking from experience. 'But be careful – patina is important to collectors, so if in doubt, don't try it.' To clean a loo, douse the toilet bowl with a mixture of baking soda and vinegar, let it linger for at least half an hour, then scrub with a toilet brush. Bicarbonate of soda sprinkled on a damp cloth will clean and deodorise surfaces. For oven cleaner, mix a cup of baking soda with enough water to make a runny paste. Spread it on the oven surfaces and let it work its magic for half an hour. Then use a scouring pad to cut through the grease.

Council tax

Don't forget to ignore the big home-based money-savers, like your mortgage deal (see page 226) and a possible council tax rebate. When council tax was launched in 1991, working out how to organise the banding was done in a bit of a rush. In the end, most properties' levy was determined by council staff driving up and down streets valuing homes from their cars. Unsurprisingly, the process led to big mistakes, with many homes put in the wrong categories. And if yours is one of them, you could be paying too much tax. Find out via the Valuation Office Agency's website at voa.gov.uk. There, you just enter your postcode and view the bandings of homes in your neighbourhood. There are eight valuation levels, from Band A (the lowest) to Band H, the highest. If homes that are similar to yours are in a different banding, yours could be wrong. If you believe that to be the case, just phone the VOA to state your case. If it does lower your banding, you can both cut the cost of your current bill and receive back-dated refunds.

Even if it's correct, you may be eligible for other discounts. Council tax bills assume two adults occupy the property as their main home, so single people can receive a discount of twenty-five per cent – but you'll have to apply for it. Some councils give furnished holiday homes a discount of between ten and fifty per cent, and you may also pay less council tax if you own an empty property where no one lives. Student halls of residence and houses lived in only by full-time students, plus armed forces accommodation and annexes like granny flats if lived in by the children of the main home's owner, are all exempt and should not pay council tax. Households with residents on certain benefits or with severe disabilities may also be eligible for a discount or exemption. See tinyurl.com/counciltaxexemptions.

Beauty

One of my best friends has to spend two thirds of her income on rent. Once she's factored in food, energy and other vital bills, she has almost nothing at all extra to spend each month. Yet she – a spa-lover – still manages to book herself in for a facial or massage every four weeks – often without paying a penny. How? By scouring the web for vouchers from sites like Wahanda – a group-buying site that specialises in spa deals (see page 27) – and signing up as a guinea pig at her local beauty college. There are tons of free and cheap beauty deals at moneysavingexpert.com, and beyond spa treats, there are plenty of ways to cut the cost of beauty. Behind the scenes, skincare specialists admit it's not crucial to roll your face in caviar, or allow Siberian snails to crawl on your face (the latest skincare revolution, apparently), or spend hundreds on potions each year to achieve smooth, younger-looking skin.

Julie Coates has spent decades seeking out the newest beauty treatments and the latest cosmetics, visiting salons and spas across the UK, and now she owns her own: The Lanes Health and Beauty, in Brighton. She says, 'There isn't a treatment or product I haven't researched and tried personally,' and she's found loads of beauty tips that women – and keen men – can carry out at home to save money, as well as ensuring we get the best out of the products we do buy by making them last longer. Here are her insider tips for saving money on looking good:

1. Instead of using expensive body scrubs (which can even irritate sensitive skin), use a pair of body exfoliating gloves (which cost as little as £1) with your normal shower gel to get baby-soft skin.

2. Push your cuticles back daily using a flannel in the shower, occasionally rubbing in your hair conditioner to soften and nourish your cuticles and save on manicures.

3. For a deep, nourishing hand treatment with ingredients from your kitchen, exfoliate your hands with olive oil and salt then apply a thick layer of olive oil, put on rubber gloves and place in hot water – the heat of the water will help the oil penetrate and condition your hands.

4. Probably the greatest 'multi-tasking' product you can have is an unscented balm – use this to condition lips, lashes, brows, cuticles and any other dry areas.

5. Instead of buying a different foundation during spring and summer – when your skin colour changes – mix your usual foundation with your daily moisturiser to give you a lighter, dewier coverage during hotter months. It will make it last longer too.

6. Add a muslin cloth to your daily cleansing routine to gently buff and exfoliate, revealing a brighter complexion without the need for extra products.

7. Keep your hair colour stronger for longer by using colour-depositing shampoos and conditioners weekly. Coloured dry-hair shampoos also disguise roots until your next haircut.

8. As a quick pick-me-up and skin tightener, submerge your face into a bowl of cold water (lots of top models do this following a red-eye flight) – it's simple, effective and almost free.

9. One thing that is worth investing in is a good daily moisturiser with an SPF, applying it to face, neck and backs of hands to counteract the harmful UV rays. Remember protection won't last all day and may need reapplying. But it'll be cheaper than a facelift in the future!

10. If your skin needs an extra boost, pierce a vitamin E capsule (a packet of one hundred costs about £5) and rub it into your skin before using moisturiser.

11. A good quality lavender oil can be used diluted in water as a cleanser, used neat as a spot treatment or dropped into a bath for a relaxing bedtime treat – three treatments in one and, as you'll only need a few drops, the bottle will last for ages.

12. Apply a thick layer of facial moisturiser whilst soaking in the bath. The steam will help the cream penetrate and nourish, acting as a DIY facial treatment.

13. A facial fake tan applied well can help disguise an uneven skin tone and reduce the need to apply so much make-up.

14. Always apply your body cream after bath or shower before your skin has completely dried; this will help seal in water as well.

15. Body brushing is one of the best beauty tips – it boosts your lymphatic system to flush out toxins and gives you a more even skin tone. A decent brush will last yonks.

16. Keep your beauty routine as simple as possible: you are more likely to stick to it. When choosing products, look for as few ingredients as possible – sometimes less is more.

17. Whilst soaking in the bath, pumice or foot file away any hard skin from feet, then afterwards apply a thick layer of body cream and pull on a pair of socks to allow the cream to soak in and nourish the skin.

18. If you want your nail polish to last longer, always apply it to a dry nail and not one that's been soaked in water. A nail expands when wet and shrinks when dry so may also cause nail polish to shrink and chip.

19. Invest in one of the gradual-tanning moisturisers that give a hint of colour – these are more hydrating and easier to apply, will hide any skin tone imperfections and act as moisturiser as well, avoiding the need to buy two products.

'Never throw away tubes of moisturiser, eye cream, foot cream, shampoo etc. just because you can't squeeze any more out. Cut the tubes open – you will usually find at least another week's worth of product left to use.' – EMILY, EAST ANGLIA

Like your home, it's a good idea to think old-school with beauty: consider your kitchen the best cosmetics lab in the world. Sure, your humble hob and fridge are never going to have the marketing budget of L'Oréal or MAC, but that doesn't mean home-made potions won't work. To find out just how good they are, check out the vault of ideas that is makeyourcosmetics.com. The site shows you how to use natural ingredients like essential oils, honey and fruit juices to make skin products, and is divided into eight categories of recipes, including 'Facial & Lip Care', 'Baby & Mommy To Be' (yup, it's an American site but the vast majority of the ingredients are still available locally), and 'Bath Soaks, Salts, Scrubs & Powders'. They're also rated by difficulty and time taken to make. One of my favourites is the 'EZ 123 Deep Moisture Hair Mask' by forum member Cecilia (just mix together an egg and three tablespoons of mayonnaise).

Fridge facials

France Baudet, owner of salon group Cannelle (cannellebeaute.com), agrees that home-made products – conjured up from ingredients that are found in most people's fridges – can have great results. Her top tips for kitchen-sourced beauty are:

- Dare to strip bare. It's the key to a fresh-faced look. Minimise heavy, dark colours and don't try to cover dark circles under your eyes with heavy foundation. Instead, try putting raw potato slices that have been chilled in the fridge on your closed eyes. Lie back, relax, and let the enzymes in the potato disperse the dark pigment, leaving your skin lighter, brighter and more radiant.

- Try making a refreshing face mask at home by mashing five strawberries and mixing with a teaspoon of cream and a teaspoon of honey. The strawberries will gently exfoliate and refresh your skin, removing impurities and even help to reduce redness, whilst the honey and cream soothe and moisturise. Careful if you have allergies.

- Some expensive spot-zapping treatments actually can dry skin, but a dab of juice from a fresh pomegranate on to a spot will zap the blemish with a mega dose of anti-oxidants.

- Mix brown sugar and honey into a paste to buff your body for smooth and silky skin.

- When you sleep very flat, water in your skin can pool around the under-eye area, which means you can wake up with puffiness. Sleep slightly propped up to avoid big swollen and puffy eyes. Cheaper than expensive eye creams.

- Before you put your feet into new open-toe shoes or sandals, apply Vaseline to prevent them rubbing and causing blisters.

- For yellowing nails caused by dark nail polishes, dip your nails in lemon juice mixed with water for a few minutes – it can help get rid of the yellow, and you don't need to use any nasty chemicals.

- With our central heating blasting, beauty products can suffer. Prevent waste by keeping your nail polish in the fridge. It prevents a gloopy thickening of the polish, meaning your polishes stay useable for longer, and guarantees a smooth application.

Meanwhile, if you're wanting to buy new make-up or other beauty products, you can't go wrong with a trip to makeupalley.com/product. It's a forum site where users post reviews of items they've bought, helping you work out whether that £30 foundation is really any better than the £5 product on sale at The Body Shop. It has thousands of reviews, with often lengthy discussions (as in, 'How can someone have that much to say about a concealer?' kind of lengthy) but also includes an at-a-glance guide to whether users would buy it again or recommend it. You have to register, but doing so is free, and over the years the site has steered me away from loads of would-have-been-a-mistake purchases towards their cheaper – or just different – alternatives.

Other ways to save money on make-up include making the most of the beauty counters in big department stores, plus Boots, Superdrug and the The Body Shop. They all offer free makeovers, which can not only provide you with a new look for free, but also provide a pretty nice way to spend an hour or so of an afternoon with a friend without spending much. They also offer free samples. Obviously it's not right to exploit this generosity, but if you're buying, say, a mascara, don't feel shy about asking for samples of the brand's latest skincare pots or other products: they will usually have trial-sized ones ready to give away. Likewise, ask local hairdressing and beauty colleges if they offer cheap or free haircuts, styles or beauty treatments.

Online, it's worth checking out a site called eyeslipsface. co.uk, or ELF. It's a New York brand which sells a huge range of make-up, with much of it available for only £1.50. If you're mad for a particular brand of designer make-up, find it at strawberrynet.com or feelunique.com at a discount. I bought a Benefit liquid foundation that cost more than £30 on the high street for less than half that at Strawberry, and it offers extra discounts when you order three or more products.

If you're about to buy lip gloss, remember that mixing a slick of Vaseline with lipstick will provide the same effect for pennies. And don't forget to make what you do buy last. Use a cotton bud to get the last dregs out of lipsticks and eye shadows, and cut apparently empty tubes open before chucking them away. If a mascara has gone dry and clumpy, rinse the brush in super-hot water (carefully) to remove all the mascara, then quickly insert it back into the container.

Swap-it shop

Why buy when you can borrow, or swap your old stuff and still get exactly what you want? The concurrent decline of the economy and rise of the internet has seen a huge number of swapping and hire websites spring up. Some specialise in dresses, others in handbags, books, baby gear, wedding dresses, furniture and more. Here are the pick of the bunch:

- Clothes. How many cheap H&M or Primark dresses can you buy for the cost of renting one designer one? If you've got a posh do coming up and need a new frock, it can work out cheaper – as well as being more eco-friendly – to hire out an Armani outfit rather than buy a 'Primarni' one. Top sites include girlmeetsdress. com (where you'll find Missoni, Marc Jacobs and 3.1 Phillip Lim, and dresses start from £29 for two nights' rental) and onenightstand.co.uk (you can visit its Chelsea, west London studio to try on if you're in town, and they even do minor alterations – prices start at £85). Another big player is wishwantwear.com (designers include Temperley, Halston Heritage, Sass & Bide or Twenty8Twelve, and prices start from £35, with either a four-day or eight-day hire). Bigwardrobe. com does the same but a bit more – it has high street fashion as well as the big guns, with Dolce & Gabbana sitting alongside Dr Martens and Gap, and the latter obviously cheaper than the former.

- Most of the above dress-swapping sites also offer costume jewellery and both designer and vintage handbags. Oh – and don't forget to keep an eye out for their sales. Since the clothes are all dry-cleaned, insured and kept in good condition, the end-of-season sales can offer generous discounts to buy the ex-hire dresses. Keen to permanently swap your unwanted clothes with others, rather than rent? Bigwardrobe.com does that too via its 'worldwide fashion exchange' page.

- For other ideas and to find out about upcoming clothes-swapping events – including local, 'real world' ones taking place around the UK – check out swishing. org, swapstyle.com and rehashclothes.com.

- Books. Every bookcase has some duplicates. Maybe it's five copies of that summer's hit blockbuster like *Eat Pray Love* or two Spanish-English dictionaries (neither ever used) or a tax handbook from 1963 (there really is a market for everything . . .). Whatever you've got and don't want, there's a cheap way to turn them into books you do want to read: swap 'em. Visit bookmooch.com or readitswapit.co.uk, where you can switch any books you've already read (or frankly don't want to) for those that you do. Almost 400,000 books – from *The Help* and *The Book Thief* to poetry, maps, and sport biographies – are listed on readitswapit.co.uk. You just log on, list books you have but no longer want, and wait for swap requests. Once received, search through the wannabe-swapper's list of books and see if there's anything you like. The only cost is postage (just over £1 for the average paperback). You can also list books you want to read, and when someone makes them available, the (free) site will let you know.

- Skills. It's not just stuff you can swap: if you're a brilliant greetings-card maker but really need a box of hand-made cookies, swap your skills. Sign up at a site like swapaskill.com or skillsbox.com and you'll tot up credits for your own work. So when you translate a letter for someone or cook or provide data entry or anything else, you earn credits which mean that in the future someone will do your DIY or accounts or something else.

- Tickets. Have a misguided relative who bought you Coldplay concert tickets when what you really, really wanted was New Order? Tap into swapmyticket.co.uk. It's a ticket exchange for music, theatre, festivals and sports events. But take care to avoid fraud by swapping the tickets face to face and never handing over cash or tickets until you've checked the ones you're getting are genuine.

- Kids. OK, you don't want to swap the kids, but you might want to exchange their stuff. For top places to do so, see page 108.

- Bags. If a vestige of your old, money-splurging life is an addiction to handbags or jewellery, you don't have to give that up just because you're saving money. You're going to have to be imaginative about it. Those fifty bags hanging off the back of your bedroom

door because you no longer love them? They can
be swapped for something more now. Just think of
swapping as the new shopping: myhandbagswap.com
is great for bags, but, before shelling out, check that
anything that's claiming to be designer comes with the
receipt or certificate that proves its authenticity.

- Don't go all virtual. A big fat caveat to all the above
  website recommendations: never overlook the real
  world. The local community outside your front
  door hosts a cornucopia of sharing, swapping and
  therefore money-saving ideas. Local libraries, charities,
  churches, schools, nurseries etc. often host swapping
  events. Some might involve a charitable donation,
  others are just in the name of being green or money-
  saving. In London, for example, mrsbears.co.uk lists
  regular swapping events. ('Feeling the pinch in the
  current climate, Mrs Bear's clothes swapshop is themed
  on a World War II "make do and mend" ethos, the
  simple idea being you can exchange your unwanted
  clothing, shoes or accessories with someone else's'.)

- Or arrange a swap yourself. If you're a member of a
  book club, introduce a swapping element so fellow
  members who've enjoyed other books pass them on,
  and you all get new reads for free. Likewise, get to
  know your neighbours and see if any are interested
  in swapping or sharing, just like the theory behind
  swapping sites such as rentmyitems.com. Since you'll
  only use a lawnmower or leaf blower for a few days
  each year, these kind of appliances are easy things to
  share – and you'll probably trust your neighbour more
  than a stranger.

Transport

Unless you're walking, the cost of getting from A to B today will almost certainly be higher than it was a year ago. The amount of money it costs to run a car went up by fourteen per cent in the last twelve months, according to the RAC Report on Motoring. Drivers now have to spend an average of £6,600 a year to keep a car on the road, thanks to rising petrol prices, insurance and motor maintenance costs. The wallet-hit isn't that much better on the trains, where fares rose by up to twelve per cent in 2012 and some season tickets into London smashed through the £8,000-a-year barrier for the first time.

Even on two wheels, bike prices, maintenance fees and insurance costs are all on the increase too. But there are still ways to cut the cost, whether it's demanding compensation for terrible train service (and non-confrontationists, you can do it online), de-junking your car or splitting tickets.

Driving

You can't change the cost of fuel (unless, that is, you are an Arab oil magnate, in which case, please cut the cost of fuel) but you can make sure the stuff you're buying is the cheapest around. At petrolprices.com drivers simply tap in their postcode and are provided with a list of the lowest fuel prices within the local radius. It claims to include nearly 11,000 petrol stations in the UK and provide 8,000 daily updates. On average, users of the website save £2 per fill-up, so anyone buying fuel every week would save over £100 a year. Supermarkets also often have petrol deals, such as vouchers for money off at the pumps when you spend a certain amount in store, so keep an eye out for these. Wherever you're driving, never wait till your car's red empty tank indicator is screaming at you to fill up: doing so will leave you desperate for fuel and forced to go to the most expensive pumps, like those at motorway service stations.

'Petrol vouchers from Tesco or other supermarkets, which often offer as much as 10p off per litre if you spend over £60 on grocery shopping, are worth looking for if you do high mileage.' – BRIAN, LONDON

Right, after the cheapest fuel has been purchased, the next step is to use what's in your tank most efficiently. Motoring experts say that driving at 55mph offers the best fuel economy. And they suggest that in summer, you embrace the idea of your car as your personal sauna, because air conditioning guzzles gas and opening your windows when driving at high speeds means extra drag, which brings down fuel efficiency. When you do need something to cool down, it's usually thought to be more fuel efficient to drive with windows open when travelling at lower speeds, but closing them and switching to air con when driving faster, because the greater resistance will make you put your foot down more to make up for it.

Filling your car with a few extra passengers can save money too. It's unlikely if the extra bum is your youngest child, but lift-sharing is growing in popularity as costs rise. See page 206 to learn about saving money via sites like blablacar.com and liftshare.com. But if it's a friend on board that you're carting around the country, and you feel awkward about demanding cash, you could ask for another kind of contribution, like car snacks or lunch. Or subtly try to lure them into the forecourt shop on the pretence of picking up some chocolate – when they see your fuel bill is £60 or more, they might be shocked into coughing up some cash.

Apart from extra paying passengers, avoid carrying excess weight in your car: it makes the engine work harder and use more petrol to move. So stop driving around with that picnic rug in the boot when it's the middle of winter, and clear the back seat of unnecessary car seats and clobber when they are not in use. Dump the roof rack when it's not needed too: it might be a hassle to put on and take off, but it's heavy and will mean you're wasting fuel. Under the bonnet, using the best grade of motor oil for your engine may improve fuel efficiency. Don't rely on the manufacturer's recommendation, but ask a trusted garage expert. Get your engine serviced regularly and make sure tyres are inflated at the right pressure – a tyre that's under-inflated by only ten per cent can force a car to use considerably more fuel than it would otherwise.

Now on to you and your driving. Smooth is the buzzword: slamming down the accelerator to race away from traffic lights and then slamming on the brake a minute later uses almost a third more fuel than smooth driving, according to petrol giant Shell. So slow down early when you see traffic lights changing to red, in the hope that by the time you get there, the light will be turning green once more and you avoid the need to brake and stop completely. And speed up a little before you reach the foot of a hill, when it's safe to do so.

Use the highest gear you can without the car labouring, and avoid over-revving. If you have it, use cruise control on motorways and fast roads to help you maintain a constant speed and boost fuel consumption. Shell also advises motorists to 'avoid excess idling – it gets you nowhere but still burns fuel. Turn the engine off when you're in a queue or waiting for someone. As a rule, if you think you will be stopped for more than ten seconds, switch off your engine. And plan trips carefully to avoid the rush hour – cutting down on the time spent in the car is the easiest way to conserve fuel. To reduce driving time, combine all your short trips and errands into a single journey. Plus, if you can travel outside of peak times, you'll spend less time stuck in traffic and consume less fuel as a result.'

When it comes to cutting other car costs, there's a fine line between penny-pinching and life-endangering. Skipping an annual service could mean missing a potentially serious problem that could put you and your passengers at risk. And cars that aren't regularly maintained are more likely to have a major breakdown – which might end up far more expensive. So you've got to get the work done, but you can still keep the cost of MOTs and services down in the following ways:

- Shop around. Main dealers tend to be more expensive than local independents. But the most important part of choosing a garage is finding one you can rely on not to rip you off or skimp on sub-standard parts. So ask friends and family for recommendations. The car website Honest John also has drivers' reviews of garages (honestjohn.co.uk). And if you find (or are told) that you need to replace a part, check its list price online first before shelling out. Car magazine *Autotrader* also lists second-hand prices of parts (autopartstrader.co.uk).

- Haggle. Once you know the cost of a replacement part, use that as your starting point to politely argue the cost down. The garage will add on labour charges; could they help reduce the part's cost, or cut the cost of labour, if it's an expensive purchase? Seek out several quotes from nearby garages. Some will allow you to buy parts yourself and pay them for fitting. Whatever you agree, always get a written quote, which should cover parts, labour and VAT.

- DIY. Some things you can learn to do yourself. To check your oil, for example, switch off the engine and let it cool, open the bonnet and you'll see four tanks. One will be marked for oil (your manual should help), and you'll need to pull out its dipstick and wipe it with an old rag before putting it back. Then pull out the dipstick again and see where the level is. If it's below the minimum mark, refill it.

- Screen wash is easy too: just open the cap and, if it needs a refill, use a funnel to pour fluid up to the maximum mark. Tyre pressure can easily be checked at a petrol station – just unscrew your tyre caps, insert the forecourt's air nozzle and wait for a reading: your required level will be listed in your handbook.

• If words like dipstick have left you scratching your head, buy a book on basic car maintenance, visit haynes.co.uk or look at the myriad of car maintenance teaching videos on YouTube and on Honest John.

If your car needs an MOT, you're probably wincing and associating it with Massive Overpriced Trauma – but that's usually the cost of repairs rather than the actual test. The MOT has a maximum fee set by the government, currently at £54.85 for cars and £29.65 for motorbikes. Some garages offer cheaper deals to secure your business, but that may end up subsidising the repair costs. If a recent service or excellent DIY maintenance means you're confident about your vehicle passing the test, it may be worth booking it in for a council-run MOT, which exist to service council vehicles but accept all motors. Since they don't carry out repairs, they have no incentive to fail your car. Contact your local council to ask for your nearest centre.

Before booking the MOT, help your car to pass its test – and avoid the expense of a re-test – by carrying out some basic checks on the most common causes of failure. Test your lights with the help of a friend telling you if they are coming on, or use a reflective shop window. If any of the bulbs don't work, new ones only cost a few pounds to replace and are usually fairly easy to change – see your manual. (By the way, if you've lost your manual, major manufacturers now make them available for free online, and even older vehicles' manuals may have been uploaded by other owners – worth a Google.)

Windscreen wipers are another easy fix: they must be in working condition and the blades need to be good enough to clear the screen. Check the tread on your tyres: the legal minimum is 1.6mm, which is about the depth of a 20p coin, and look for any tears or bulges. Remember to include the spare tyre in your tests too, and if any tyres need replacing, buy one from the cheapest reputable source before taking your car to its MOT. Other easy parts to check yourself include the mirrors – must be securely attached – and windscreen: no chips. Make sure the brake fluid, screen wash and oil are all topped up, and all the seat belts work too.

When your car is due a service, compare prices at a few main dealers and garages in your area and haggle to get the best quote. Some will offer discounts on parts and labour if a car is over three years old, but only if you ask. One way to cut costs is to take your own oil – you can shave as much as £100 off the cost of a service by taking in your own oil, which is available for less than £10 a litre from places like Halfords and supermarkets or cash and carries such as Costco.

If you're considering buying a new car, see page 41. Or, avoid all of these costs and worries by selling your car and joining a car club. Try zipcar.co.uk or citycarclub.co.uk to see if either are up and running in your area and examine the costs.

Cutting back on courier, moving or delivery costs

Soaring petrol costs mean that if you need to shift a bulky piece of furniture, car, eBay purchase or other hefty item, such as a teenager's possessions from home to uni, it can now be cheaper to use a delivery service than do it yourself in your own vehicle. Opting for a courier service or even a man with a van may still be expensive, but check out shiply.com for potentially lower fees. It's an online marketplace for goods transport that matches up lorries, vans and couriers with space on board, with people who need something delivered.

So all those massive lorries taking up motorway space with empty loads on their way back to the depot can move your belongings. It's a simple idea: you advertise the items you need to move on the website, including the timescale, size and pick-up and delivery address, and hauliers or couriers who are already making that journey or a similar one, and who have spare space on board, bid to carry out your move. You can then pick the cheapest bid – as well as view other users' reviews and recommendations of their services – and save money.

The site has a price estimate calculator so you can gauge average charges. It claims average users save seventy-five per cent off the cost of traditional haulage and courier fees. You can research companies using the site's feedback rating system and check HGV licences by clicking the 'operator search' button at tan.gov.uk, but you should still always make sure the company has proper insurance and provides copies of policy documents.

Train tickets

Tracking down the cheapest train ticket used to require a forensic ability to sift through endless apex leisure super-advance express direct leisure pronto (I could go on . . .) fares in order to find the one you actually wanted (generally just a reasonable ticket that would get you to your location within two hours, with a seat, and without being so expensive as to make walking to the destination seem worth considering for at least thirty seconds). But since National Rail had a go at simplifying the ticket-buying process back in 2010, there are fewer ticket types and it's now a lot easier to work out what to buy. Prices, however, still oscillate wildly. As with fliers on budget airlines, passengers sitting next to each other on a train still regularly discover that one has spent as much as a few hundred pounds more than the other for the very same journey. What follows is a guide to making sure you're always the one paying less.

1. The most important money-saving step is to book in advance. Twelve weeks is usually the magic number – it's the time when operators release their new tickets. After that, train times are confirmed, and advance tickets begin to appear on Network Rail's journey planner with full details of availability (see nationalrail.co.uk).

2. If there's a route you regularly take, sign up with thetrainline.com's ticket alert email and it will tell you as soon as your desired tickets go on sale. Since advance tickets are restricted to specific services, you'll

need to know exactly which day and train you want to travel on.

3. Don't forget that advance fares don't have to be booked months ahead of travel. Doing so will boost your chance of buying the very cheapest ticket, but even booking the night before your journey – or sometimes on the same day, but at home with an e-ticket purchased a few hours before departure – can trigger a big saving when compared with buying at the ticket office minutes before departure.

4. The cheapest tickets are for midweek, off-peak travel, after 10 a.m. and not between 5 p.m. and 7 p.m.

Once you've decided roughly what ticket you're looking for, the next port of call should be nationalrail.co.uk. Here you can work out which train company runs the route, plus your timetable and fare options. With that info in hand, your next task is to visit the operator's website direct to check for any special deals: some run £1 specials at particular times of year, or if they are facing a slump in demand, for example. If the offer is cheap enough, and it's possible, you might decide to bring your journey time forward, or back, to save money.

Look at all of the ticket-buying options: sometimes it costs less to buy two single fares rather than one return ticket. It's worth looking at routes via discount brand Megatrain too – go to megabus.com/uk and click 'train' on the drop-down menu when searching for routes. Its fares start at £1 and, although they are usually at less popular times, they cover over a hundred destinations and the seats are on trains run by South West Trains, East Midlands Trains and Virgin Trains.

It's worth checking to see if other booking sites like thetrainline.com and raileasy.co.uk have cheaper tickets, but note they do have booking fees (usually £1, and the trainline.com also charges £3.50 for using a credit card), so remember to factor those costs in. Delivery may also be extra, be remember you can opt to pick up a ticket from a machine on a station concourse for free.

Perhaps the least known, but potentially most money-saving ticket-buying strategy is to split your ticket. For a return trip from London to Manchester, for example, it may work out cheaper to buy a single ticket from London to Stoke-on-Trent and then another from Stoke to Manchester, than purchasing one return fare for the whole journey. There's no need to change trains either, as long as the train calls at the stations at which you're splitting the journey. It sounds complicated, but the website splityourticket.co.uk does the work for you and will tell you if savings are possible for your journey.

Splitting a ticket can be most beneficial for anyone travelling on a long train journey which includes some peak travel. By splitting a ticket, you need only pay the higher, peak-time fare for the part of the route that you're travelling at peak times. So say the journey began at 9 a.m. and was scheduled to finish at 1 p.m., it would be possible to only pay for the first hour at peak rate, triggering big savings.

Further discounts are available via rail cards. These cost £28 a year, or £65 for a three-year pass, and offer a third off all rail fares including both standard and first-class advance tickets. They are available to those aged under twenty-six (the 16–25 Railcard), those over sixty (the Senior Railcard) and to families and groups (the Family and Friends Railcard, which saves users a third off adult ticket prices and sixty per cent off kids' fares). With the Family and Friends card, users need to be travelling in a group with between one and three adults, and one to four children aged five to fifteen. (Kids under five go free anyway.) A Network Railcard, which only covers the south-east of England, gives a discount of up to a third off journeys within London and its surrounding area. It covers up to four adults who travel after 10 a.m. on weekdays or at any time on weekends, plus up to four children. The Disabled Persons Railcard (which is slightly cheaper than the rest, at £20 per year or £54 for three years) cuts a third off both the holder's fare plus that of an adult companion. To find out more about eligibility check out: disabledpersons-railcard.co.uk.

Commuting

Anyone buying a season ticket for a regular journey can work out the price with the nationalrail.co.uk journey planner. Take a deep breath – the cost is likely to be significant, making it all the more worthwhile to play around with the above options, particularly ticket-splitting if possible. And remember if your train experiences any delays – usually of more than thirty minutes – you can claim back some of the cost. Keep hold of your ticket and pick up a reclaim form from station concourses, or log into the route operator's website. There's more info on who to contact and how best to do it via the commuter-run site trainrefunds.co.uk.

In London, anyone using the Tube should have an Oyster card, which makes journeys much cheaper than paying with cash. Under-eighteens and students can receive further discounts on journeys with special Oyster cards (tinyurl.com/tflstudent). Note that with a pay-as-you-go Oyster, it will be cheaper to travel your whole journey by Tube than taking a Tube and then a bus – even if doing so is quicker or more direct – because there are no free transfers and it's seen as breaking your journey. With journeys priced according to zone, it's worth looking at a Tube map and checking whether getting off one stop earlier could save you money – in central London, many stops are easy walking distance from one another. Claim a refund on any Tube journey struck by delays of fifteen minutes or longer via the site tfl.gov.uk.

Cycling

On the face of it, cycling looks like the cheapest form of transport around, apart from using your own two feet. But as bike riding has gone from minority sport to mainstream mode of moving around cities, the costs have risen, from pricey bike options to super-robust locks and insurance, as well as maintenance charges.

If you don't have a bike, but would be able to (and want to) cycle to work if you owned one, and you need a financial incentive, check out cycletoworkcalculator.com. It works out how much cash and time you are wasting on your current commute, and how much switching to a bike could save you. And if that calculation convinces you – or you're just after two wheels to ride on during your leisure time – when buying a bike you'll want to work out how to get the best value out of your investment. Bikes aren't worth scrimping on: the better the bike, the more you'll enjoy riding it – and I speak on this matter with some authority, as the one-time owner of a £49 bum-shaker from Toys 'R' Us. But they don't have to cost a bomb: when I finally upgraded, I found a £500 bike reduced to £300 in a big sale at my local store, and I enjoy riding it.

Visit several shops, and find an advisor you're happy with to talk you through the options. Most bike shops in the UK are members of the Association of Cycle Traders and will have mechanics with Cytech qualifications. Note that if you buy a bike online, you'll usually be expected to assemble the cycle yourself.

'When visiting anywhere around the UK or, in fact, abroad – if you can, then walk or hire a bike. You'll see more for less money.' –
ARJAN, BIRMINGHAM

A major way to make savings on your purchase is via the government-backed Cyclescheme (cyclescheme.co.uk/ getting-a-bike). It allows you to buy a bike tax free, which will mean saving up to fifty per cent of the cost for taxpayers. You can use Cyclescheme to buy almost any bike from one of 1,700 independent bike shops and big chains, but you'll need your employer to have signed up to the scheme. If they haven't, it's easy to do so and the above site has information on how they can do it.

If budget is crucial and you just want to be able to afford any bike at all, opt for a second-hand cycle. Local bike shops should be able to help, or monitor the options on Gumtree or eBay. Before buying, as with any second-hand goods, you should check the bike hasn't been stolen by tapping its frame number into the national property register backed by the police, Immobilise (immobilise.com).

If you're new to two wheels, or haven't been on them since childhood, sign up for some free cycle tutoring. It's available for both adults at kids across the UK – check out cycletraining.co.uk to find one near you.

Once you've bought a bike, you'll need to organise regular services to keep it road-worthy. If there's a branch of Evans Cycles near you, book in to one of its free bi-monthly bike maintenance classes to learn how to do it yourself. Or if your employer is part of the aforementioned Cycle-to-Work scheme, ask if they have a discount scheme at a nearby cycle workshop. Many organise free safety checks, repairs and maintenance sessions.

I used to visit a high-street cycling store for an annual bike service, but ended up feeling the same as I do each year at my car's service: as if, as soon as I walked out of the shop, the blokes inside were laughing at me for just how much I had been taken for a ride (no pun intended). Since my knowledge of gears ends at the fact they make it a hell of a lot easier to get up the hill at the end of my road, I never knew whether to trust mechanic Mick who promised I really did need that new brake pad/inner tube/etc.

So I asked friends for recommendations and eventually found a local independent cycle shop where I trust the staff. Although the initial prices might seem higher than those of a chain, my experience has been that the independent shop is happy to tighten bolts and repair unaligned gears for free in between services, so it works out cheaper overall. Another option is to call out a bloke-on-a-bike, aka a repair service that comes to your house. These guys tend to be cheaper in winter, when there's less work around, so for year-round cyclists, the cold months are a good time to book in.

To avoid being stitched up worse than a posh leather saddle, as with car parts you should check online to see how much bicycle parts cost before agreeing to pay for them. Or you could try buying parts, yourself and watch basic videos online that teach you how to carry out the necessary work.

Rising bike theft means that insurance will be worthwhile for most regular cyclists. Compare the options via a comparison site.

Walk

Don't forget the cheapest form of transport around: the two plates of meat at the end of your legs. In London, getting off the Tube one stop early and walking the rest of the route can mean travelling through one fewer zone and wipe hundreds off the cost of an annual Travelcard. And if you need an incentive, walking a mile rather than taking the bus or using a car will save you enough to afford at least three chocolate bars. And you'll have burnt off the calories too.

Walking saves on parking fees, and, if you do enough of it and go speedily, perhaps even gym membership, as well as improving your health. If you still need convincing – or just want some route guidance – check out walkit.com, or download its app on a smartphone. The site allows you to just type in your city and where you are or want to walk to, and it will provide a route map which includes journey time if you're a fast, medium or slow walker, as well as calorie burn, step count and how much carbon you are saving. There are also suggestions for local walks – and the site, like walking, is free to use.

PART 3
Making it
Money-making ideas

Do you want to earn £100s extra a year from the comfort of your own home? Do you want to do so in your own time, and whilst being your own boss?

YES, IF SOMEONE SAID THIS TO ME I too would think it sounded like one of those dodgy posters taped to the side of a lamp post on an A road. But it is possible, and in a completely legal way: anyone with a home computer and internet really can find dozens of easy – though, admittedly, sometimes pretty darn boring – ideas to earn extra cash, and you can do it whenever you have some free time, whether it's at three in the morning or four in the afternoon, when your boss has gone into a meeting or baby is down for a nap.

They're not all online – you'd be shocked at how much you can sell your unwanted clobber for at places like car boot sales, or make from renting out a spare room, even if it's just between Monday and Friday, or even selling a juicy part of your life story to newspapers. But many of them are internet-based, to the extent that much of this chapter reads like an (I hope more interesting) extrapolation of the 'favourites' list on my computer. Things like filling in online surveys, cashing in on ads on your own website, renting your belongings out, turning your home into a movie set, flogging even non-working phones, selling your photos to image agencies, seeking out forgotten bank accounts and getting paid to be a mystery shopper. Oh, and read on to find out how I once sold a cardboard box online for a grand total of £6. I then looked into some of the weirder sales on eBay and discovered bog-standard plastic carrier bags and a pair of old socks, which from the photo looked holier than the Archbishop of Canterbury, actually selling for a couple of quid. People are weird, and they buy weird things – exploit that.

Whilst it feels pretty satisfying to find new ways to penny-pinch on the things we buy without noticing a difference, it's even more rewarding to find new and easy ways to make a bit of extra cash in your spare time. Some ideas – like selling your crafty talents – might involve hobbies and seem more like play than work, others are very easy ways to fill in spare moments in front of a computer, and still more will quickly become part of your daily routine.

During a spell of joblessness I once spent a week entering competitions online. I skipped past massive, popular winathons like holidays on *This Morning* or newspaper prizes, but logged on to esoteric sites for local journals, small e-tailers and the makers of random foodstuffs. Pick unpopular ones and it can pay off – over the next few weeks, prizes started dribbling in – ten *Lonely Planet* travel guides, a 'pro' tennis racquet (followed by immediate disappointment on arriving at the sorting office to discover said 'pro' was an eight-year-old Junior champion and the racquet about the size of my forearm), personalised notepaper . . . Hardly enough to quit the job search, but anything I didn't want made a nice addition to my present cupboard or went on eBay.

Nowadays I fill in online surveys with half an eye whilst

watching TV in the evenings – making an easy fiver if you do enough – and many of our 'date nights' are paid for by mystery shopping companies. Take care: you don't want to throw away your internet and home privacy by giving everyone your personal details in return for just a few pennies. My advice is to set up an alternative email address to avoid getting your main one chock full of surveys and perhaps junk if you forget to tick the 'privacy please' box. Always look out for that option, though, and only give away details such as your address to reputable companies.

My other top tip is to track all your extra earnings. Not just because if you do enough of them you'll need to tell the taxman (you will: see page 220), but because this is like modern-day pin money and, if you can afford to do so, it's nice to blow a little of the extra cash on a treat that you might not be able to – or let yourself – afford otherwise at the end of each year.

Money-making ideas

Earn as you learn

Brainiacs should keep an eye on the vacancy list at Any Question Answered (aqa.63336.com). It's a site where people pay to text in questions – ranging from 'why is the sky blue?' to 'what is the meaning of life?' to 'is it dinner time yet?' – and it pays freelancers to answer them. The pay per question is low – usually about 30p for each one answered – but it can be interesting, and doesn't take long to answer most.

Want to use your brain for bigger problems? Check out innocentive.com, where businesses post problems that are foxing them, and ordinary Joes can earn serious amounts of money by answering them. A lot of them are really techy: 'Seeking Cyclazinium Salts', is the introduction to one firm's request, with a $600 fee for each one (whatever one is) that is found. But some are creative, or business-orientated ('work out systems to monitor institutional corruption' – for an $8,000 reward). It's more lucrative than doing a sudoku . . .

Elsewhere online you can pocket cash for filling in surveys. At some sites, the earnings amount to only pennies, but at others an in-depth survey, including recording your activities on a daily basis, can net participants £100 or more. There are lots of firms looking for respondents, including yougov.com (the pay is low, usually less than £1 per survey, but they're very quick); valuedopinions.co.uk (usually pays between £1 and £5 for completed surveys, although recipients are paid via vouchers, not cash); globaltestmarket.com (short surveys, cheques paid from the US); uk.toluna.com (participants earn gift vouchers and site rewards); and panelbase.net (usually up to £2 per survey, plus £3 on offer for each recommended friend).

And if you have your own website, think about adding adverts to it so you'll get paid every time someone clicks on your site. Google's Adsense (google.co.uk/adsense), clickbank (clickbank.com) and Amazon's Associates (affiliate-program.amazon.co.uk) are the most popular. Your earnings will obviously depend on your site's popularity.

Rent your stuff

Every household has unwanted stuff, the kind that you don't want right now but aren't ready to permanently part with. For parents, it might be bags of old clothes that no longer fit the oldest child but are still a metre too long on the younger one. For others it could be that breadmaker you're definitely going to start using to bake ciabatta . . . any day now. Or it might just be the lawnmower and barbecue that you probably don't use for 360 days a year. Or that spare foldaway bed that you squash into the living room only once a year for cousin Zelda's annual visit. You don't want to get rid of that stuff. Cousin Zelda might complain, for one thing. And what if one day you finally fancy that home-baked ciabatta? But there's a money-making, space-saving solution: rent it out.

The internet is an easy way to do it. Dozens of rent-your-stuff sites have sprung up in recent years, including rentmyitems.com and zilok.com/uk. Most of the websites allow users to sign up for free, whereupon you start listing items at fees starting from £1. When I was last logged in, listings included a hammer (£3 a day), uplighting for a wedding (£75 a day – and I'm tempted) and ceramic rollers (£3.50 a day). Renters also pay a deposit, and all users are rated by others based on their experiences, eBay-style, so it's easy to check out their credentials. The sites suggest working out your goods' rental prices by dividing the cost of the item by thirty and then adding twenty-five per cent. Have a prowl through your home and see what you could use to make money.

Offline there are other kinds of rental or swapping opportunities: try advertising your goods at a local newsagent, church, community centre, library or, for parents, at a nearby childcare hub, school or nursery. You may need to set up your own safeguards and ask locally for recommendations.

Rent your bigger stuff

How about starting with a room? The lodger is back. Austerity Britain has been the perfect incubation environment for the resurgence in renting out rooms. If your home is near a university campus, you could find a student to pay you rent. If it's near a jobs hot spot or station, someone looking to cut their daily commute might fit the bill. Close to an airport or nightlife spot, and you might secure a member of cabin crew or night-shift worker looking for a bed near their base. Big listings sites include spareroom.co.uk, where you can post for free or pay more for a premium listing, and uk.easyroommate.com, where it's free to post an ad but communicating with a potential renter involves fees (these depend on the size of your property). Other places to advertise including local libraries and newsagent windows.

If you're just looking for a weekday lodger and want your home to be your own on the weekends, check out mondaytofriday.com. It costs £29.95 for a three-month listing. For more lucre, but potentially more responsibility, try contacting a local further education college or language school to see if they're looking for host families.

Remember, for your own safety, it's crucial to secure at least two references for your potential lodger and to follow them up; ideally ask for an employer and previous landlord's reference. It's worth drafting a contract to protect both sides – SpareRoom has some that are accredited by the National Landlords' Association at spareroom.co.uk/content/info-landlords/lodger-agreement. Outline exactly what's included (such as washing for an extra fee, use of the internet, utility bills, Sky, etc.) and your household rules.

Make sure you don't fall foul of the taxman. The government's rent-a-room scheme allows earnings of up to £4,250 a year (from which reasonable expenses incurred in letting out the room, such as advertising it, can be deducted) for renting a room without having to pay tax. But go beyond that and you will be liable.

Another rental opportunity that has grown hugely in recent years as the economy has, well, let's put it nicely and say faltered, is renting out your driveway or parking space. The easiest way to do this is via parkatmyhouse.com and yourparkingspace.co.uk. Homeowners with spaces near London stations or sports stadia charge as much as £12 a day. Others rent their spaces on a weekly or monthly basis. Just don't be greedy – a lot of homeowners complain of no demand for their spaces, but it's because they're asking too much. Few commuters will spend more than a fiver a day on parking, and even that's a fair whack; price fairly to ensure a healthy demand.

If you skipped over the last paragraph because you do have a car and you need that driveway, there's still another money-making opportunity. Your car is sure to be a major expense, and since you're almost certainly not using your vehicle all day, every day, consider making some extra money out of it when it's not in use. Share your petrol bills on long journeys or regular commutes by organising a lift-share with friends or colleagues or via a site like blablacar. com or liftshare.com. Register on these sites either a regular commute or a long journey you're planning on making, and wait to see if you can secure some extra passengers to help pay your way. Someone making a ten-mile journey three times a week would save £345 a year by sharing it with one other passenger who paid £2.48 per trip, according to liftshare. And it helps the environment as well as your pocket: taking just one other car off the road would be the equivalent of offsetting seventeen trees.

Another idea for drivers is to visit car rental site whipcar. com, where you can hire out your own vehicle to others. The site checks cars and drivers with the government's licensing body, the DVLA, to make sure they are not stolen or dodgy, and requires credit card details of those involved on both sides of the agreement for extra safety. It also offers a special insurance policy. Earnings depend on the size and marque of your car, plus its location, but usually start at around £5 an hour; most motorists, however, offer hirers bulk deals on daily and weekly rentals too.

Elsewhere in your home, if you've got an empty loft hoarding little but dust, or large storage cupboards, you could turn the unused space into cash via storemates.co.uk or sharemystorage.com. These sites match people who have stuff to store with homeowners who have spare space. A locked garage in Hertfordshire is being rented out for £25 a week; a 250-square-foot cellar in Cumbria is bringing in £15 a week. Storemates is free for a basic listing, but charges an admin fee of two weeks' rental. Sharemystorage is also free to list, then charges one week's rental. Both sites have sample contracts that renters/owners can sign, as well as advice about the implications for your home insurance policy.

Other parts of your dwelling that could provide some extra ker-ching include your garden: homeowners on campinmygarden.com earn about £10–£20 per person per night for renting out a bit of their garden as a camping site. Many charge more for allowing campers into homes for a shower or even a hot breakfast. The most popular locations are those near music festivals or sports events. Or if your garden is too much for you to take on, consider renting it out to a friend or neighbour as an allotment, either for money or for a food-swap: they give you a certain amount of the produce.

Or maybe your whole home is Hollywood-worthy. This doesn't mean your kitchen has to look like Brad Pitt's: production companies are often scouting for sets for films and TV shows, so it's worth checking out if yours fits the bill.

The main requisite is that the rooms must be large enough to accommodate a crew of a dozen or so people. Day rates can be as much as £2,500 – but although that sounds loads, you should be aware that the crew will take over your home entirely, and some report horror stories of ruined homes. It can sour your relationship with neighbours: when one of ours had an enormous TV film crew in situ for six months, the lorries didn't go down well with the locals. So make sure you have a contract to guarantee the place is left in the condition it's in when you hand over the keys, and talk to neighbours first. If you're keen to get involved, either contact production companies directly – with good photos – or register with a location agency like locationworks. com, lavishlocations.com, amazingspace.co.uk or location-collective.co.uk. Using an agency will mean payments, contracts and insurance are all organised on your behalf – but obviously will involve fees.

How to sell your home on eBay

Well, not quite your home, just all the rubbish that you don't really need, which is threatening to burst out of your drawers and cupboards next time you turn your head. Go through each room and pile up anything you don't need or want in a corner. Unless it's holey underwear or a mouldy cheese sandwich you're looking at, don't dismiss anything as un-eBay-able. I recently sold a cardboard box on the online auction house for £4, plus £2 postage. I've no idea why the buyer bought it, but people are strange and will buy almost anything, so be imaginative. And why pay the council to remove an old armchair when you can find people on eBay who'll pay for it? Even if it only brings in a tenner, it all adds up. Here are the rules of eBay de-cluttering:

- Pick a free listing day. These pop up every few weeks and mean that you won't have to pay to advertise your item (although eBay does take a cut of all sold prices: the 'final value' fee is ten per cent of the sale price, up to a maximum of £40, on all auctions). If you're selling with a starting price of 99p or less, you won't ever have to pay to list.

- Take your time with the advert. This is the most important part of the sales process. Compose your wording carefully (if it's a branded good, advertise that fact; if it's brand new, make sure that's obvious) and take the best picture that you can. For more valuable items, it's worth paying extra to post a few pictures and a more detailed item description. Include as much info as you can, including size, brand, design, price when new, what's good about your item, the reason you're selling it (if relevant – when I post anything decorative I refer to my upset at having to sell it), size, condition, material, etc. Be sure to use the right spelling to guarantee people searching for your item can find it. And always be honest about the condition of your goods – apart from the obvious point of decency, doing otherwise risks earning you a poor review, which will hit your ability to secure future sales.

- Set your price with care. Research what similar items

have sold for in the past, and don't overestimate your item's value: remember this is an auction site. Check out get4it.co.uk for detailed statistics that will help you to work out the best starting price.

- Be careful with your timing. Auctions tend to last for a set number of days, but get most popular as the deadline approaches. So make sure your sale doesn't end at two in the morning. And for higher-value items, think about the best time of year to sell too. Bikes and tents will be in higher demand in spring, heaters and hot water bottles in December.

Empty your 'man drawer'

Old mobiles and other electrical gadgets that have piled up in the 'man drawer' – comedian Michael McIntyre's term for that bedside electrical graveyard for junk and other things 'we feel we may need in the future' – could well be eBay-able. But it could be easier to sell unwanted electrical goods via recycling sites like mazumamobile.com or tescomobilerecycle.com. All you have to do is enter your phone's (or other device's) details on the sites, including whether it's working or not (even broken ones are accepted), and they will offer you a fee, and, if you accept it, send out a free envelope or Jiffy bag for you to post back your mobile. Then the company will post a cheque, or pay it into your bank account.

There are a plethora of sites out there and they all pay out different amounts for different goods. Find out which site will pay you the most for your device using the comparison table at moneysavingexpert.com. Some sites also accept other gadgets like satnavs and music players, cameras and laptops. Note, though, that whilst these sites are very convenient, to earn the absolute maximum returns, research by consumer group Which? found auction site eBay or high street retailers such as Cex (find a branch at uk.webuy.com/stores) often offered more generous sums and were faster at processing payments in some cases. So compare the sales values before going for one site.

Or, for old electronics and other devices that you'd love to use but can't remember how to, and have lost the instruction booklet for, check out usersmanualguide.com.

Books

Elsewhere in your house, have you got over-full bookcases? If you've a large quantity of books, or any that you think might be of significant value, ask a local second-hand bookshop for a valuation. Or try out Amazon – it's not just for buying. Sign up to its marketplace function, then type in your books' ISBN numbers (found on one of the first few pages) and a brief description of its condition, and Amazon will add all the other details, including user reviews, and sell your second-hand books on your behalf. It charges 86p per item as a completion fee, plus a closing fee that's a percentage of the sales price for each item sold: 11.5 per cent for electronics and photo items, or 17.25 per cent for anything else. Or to sell cheap paperbacks, online second-hand bookshop greenmetropolis.com pays sellers £3 for every book sold – although that does include postage, so the final amount you earn might not be very high.

Focus groups

It's not quite as easy as online surveys – for one thing, you'll usually have to leave the house, but joining market research panels is usually much more lucrative than online surveys. Focus group companies usually pay between £20 and £200 to people who respond to questions or form part of a discussion group, usually about new products. I went to one a few months ago that involved reading an instruction leaflet about a new diarrhoea drug for two minutes, followed by being quizzed on what I'd understood by it for another three minutes, and was then swiftly given a cheque for £50. Sure, it's wasn't the most entertaining way to spend five minutes, but it was pretty easy lucre.

Most focus group organisers will only let you participate in a few discussions per year, and of those, screening questions will mean you're only eligible for some, so it's worth signing up to several companies. Find local ones in your phone directory, or try national firms such as sarosresearch.com, indiefield.net, the Grapevine Panel from fieldinitiatives.co.uk, focus4people.com, focusforce. net and claret-uk.com.

Sell your photos

Fancy yourself as a bit of a David Bailey – or always thought the stock pictures you see on websites, in magazines and on TV are easy to replicate? Prove it: sell your photos. Photo banks like istockphoto.com are always looking for shots to illustrate articles and more, and you'll earn royalties for each one sold. iStockphoto pays contributors a royalty of fifteen per cent each time their pictures are downloaded, or if you use it as your exclusive agent, you can secure a higher royalty rate of between twenty-two per cent and forty-five per cent. The site has detailed information about what it's looking for in photos (or logos, videos and flash animation, which it also accepts) at istockphoto.com. Similar sites include alamy.com and crestock.com.

Sell your story

If you haven't got any nice pictures to flog, what about telling people about your life experiences? I'm not suggesting you turn that 'clubbing night from hell with three drunk friends continuously trying to flush your hair down the loo' experience from fifteen years ago into a novel: apart from anything else, that's rarely a route to riches.

But magazines and newspapers are always on the lookout for shocking stories, and many will pay to hear you tell yours if it's dramatic enough and fits with what they're looking for. To do so, contact newspapers and magazines directly – most list a phone number to 'tell us your story' on their pages, or alternatively speak to an agency such as featureworld.co.uk or talktothepress.co.uk, who will liaise with publications on your behalf. Note most publications will demand a photo too. Most women's magazines and newspapers will pay upwards of £200 for a story that makes a long feature, but if it's very unusual or fits in with a story that's elsewhere in the news, fees can reach £1,000 or more. Using an agent will mean they take a cut – but could make it more likely to arrive on the right person's desk.

Sell yourself for a fiver

No, not like that – this isn't that kind of book. Just check out the website fivesquids.co.uk and post an offer to do anything you're good at, and users might just agree to pay you a fiver to do it. People's offers include 'I will draw you as a cartoon or anime styled character for £5', 'I will translate anything from English to Russian for £5', 'I will break up with your boyfriend/girlfriend for you for £5'. (The latter description goes on: 'Having travelled the world and been in many relationships, I see myself as a bit of a relationship ending pro. I will contact your "worse half" by mail or phone or both and give them the news. Please note that this service is serious and will end your relationship so please do some "soul searching" before committing to buy. Note: Please message me before buying so I can assess the job.') Another says: 'I will make 2 Individual Message Valentines cards for £5' (which left me pondering: surely most people only need one . . . ?). If you're a crafty one and can make beautiful cards, decorations or other hand-made items, check out etsy.com, see page 52.

Home work

There are plenty of ways to secure bigger projects that you can carry out from home online: just sell your skills. Brilliant at cake-baking? You could be paid to make someone's wedding cake. A whizz at Photoshop? Find work editing a big corporation's staff photos to make them look pro. Maybe you're a talented songwriter, and could compose a company's jingle for a local radio ad. Where do you find projects like this? Check out peopleperhour.com, freelancer.com or studentgems.com – the latter is aimed at students but you don't have to be one to sign up for the work. The pay will depend on the duration and skills required for each role, as well as how many other people are bidding for it. It's free to join the sites, and to bid on work, but a fee will be taken out of your total earnings for each piece of work.

The bog standard

Don't forget the usual ways to make money. If you work, ask your boss for a pay rise – well, if you don't ask, you don't get – or see if you can secure some paid overtime. Think about taking on extra jobs in your spare time like babysitting, dog-walking, tutoring or house-sitting. And don't forget to claim any compensation you might be due for the recent string of mis-selling scandals from banks and other providers: see page 239. Likewise, it's worth checking whether you could be due a tax rebate from HMRC (to do so, find out whether you've been on the wrong tax code using HMRC's online code calculator).

Better than the back of the sofa

Ensure, too, that you haven't forgotten about any old savings pots or funds that you might have set up decades ago and overlooked having moved house or jobs over the years. It's really easy to find any cash that you might still have lying around in your name in old bank accounts, premium bonds or investments funds – just visit mylostaccount. org.uk. The site is a joint venture between the British Bankers' Association, the Building Societies Association and National Savings & Investments. When visiting it, fill in as many details as you can, including your past addresses, and it will track down missing money in any of forty-three banks, fifty-two building societies or premium bonds from NS&I. To do the same for missing pension pots, contact the government's free pension-hunting service at thepensionservice.gov.uk, or for old unit trusts, visit investmentuk.org.

Get paid for shopping

No one will ever be made into a millionaire just by mystery shopping, but it's easily the best 'extra' job I've ever done. Reporting back to bosses about experiences in shops and restaurants is an easy and sometimes fun way to make a few quid. I once 'mystery shopped' a big gym chain, for which I received three months' membership free, an eyebrow-waxing session (you had to try the spa, and that was the cheapest and only option they'd pay me back for: admittedly, it wasn't so fun) plus £100 for my efforts. Other mystery shopping options include hotel stays and even flights. But more usually, it will be testing out pizza deliveries and petrol stations. The theory is that bosses are always worried about whether Derek on the till in Derby is providing 'service with a smile' when he flogs burgers, BlackBerrys or anything else, so they pay mystery shoppers (usually around £5) to visit Derek in store.

Although the pay isn't brilliant, the bonus is that you usually get to keep whatever you buy, so whilst a fiver won't cover much once you've travelled to, say, Pizza Hut, had a meal, written up a report (and sometimes taken secret photos), got home and emailed back the receipt, you've had a dinner for two and been paid £5 for it. And if you get lucky with a hotel, gym or petrol station assignment, so much the better.

From my mystery shopping experience (pretty much my whole three years of uni: a lot of pizza was consumed) I'd recommend that you sign up with a wide range of sites, because unless you live in a major city it will take a while for you to find jobs in your area. Sites to check out include retaileyes.co.uk, amberarch.com, gapbuster.com/mystery-shopping, tnsglobal.com, grassrootsmysteryshopping.com, bareinternational.com and retail-maxim.co.uk. And anyone twenty-five or under can pick up extra work at oldenoughtodrink.co.uk, which tests shops, supermarkets, pubs and bars to see whether they're sticking to age restrictions on things like booze, cigarettes, and DVDs.

Avon lady calling

Don't dismiss traditional extra-hours sales work as another way to make a little extra. Avon ladies and Tupperware parties have moved on; the 1950s housewives' favourite has now become a booming industry, and every year the papers have at least one colour spread of an Avon lady, or man, standing outside their five-bedroom house, next to their Porsche, all bought with Avon pounds. They may be the exception to the rule but thousands of people are still making money through selling on evenings, weekends or snatched moments during of the day. Nowadays it's not about selling cold cream or washable food containers, but hosting parties featuring anything from sex toys and body lotions to cookwear and cosmetics, and door-to-door sales or at-home parties are a flexible way to earn money. You can do it in your spare time, whenever you want, and as much as you want – although some firms will demand minimum targets, so never sign up without reading the terms. And find out if there's already a representative working in your 'patch' – if so, and they're good at it, best to either try another product, or another location.

Most sales companies like Avon work by taking a small fee from a first batch of orders, then offering a discount of around twenty per cent on the first £100 worth of sales. The discount rises as sales increase, so more sales convert into more profit. Popular offerings include Ann Summers, The Body Shop, Jamie Oliver at Home, Colour Me Beautiful cosmetics, Pampered Chef and, of course, good old Avon.

Printing money

It's not quite money for old rope, but it is for old printer cartridges. Recycling companies will pay you up to a fiver for your old printer ink holders. Rates vary depending on the brand, size and age of your printer – so shop around at cashforcartridges.co.uk or inkcycle.co.uk. If you work in an office, it's worth asking your boss or office manager what they do with their cartridges too – they will probably go through far more ink than the average household, so the earnings can mount up fast.

Extra, extra

It sounds more glamorous than the waiting-around-for-a-very-long-time reality is likely to be, but if you've got spare time and want to earn both money and bragging rights, look around for work as an extra. Unless you're friends with Simon Cowell, in which case you probably don't need the £50–£100-ish daily fee, the most common route to work as a TV or film extra is either via an agent or via an advert. These are posted in industry newspaper the *Stage* or local papers, if film and TV crews are looking for a large number of local people for things like crowd scenes. There are hundreds of extras agencies in the UK, and most ask for sign-up fees. Opt for one that takes the fee from your first pay, rather than demanding it upfront, and shop around, asking for recommendations to make sure you've found a reputable agency with plenty of work. The biggest agencies include Casting Collective, Ray Knight and Mad Dog.

Make money out of your friends

And without losing them. Thousands of companies, ranging from satellite TV providers to banks and shops, offer big discounts or even cashback to those who refer a friend to their services. Banks offer as much as £100, so if you hear of a friend who's looking for a new current account, phone provider, breakdown cover or more, offer to send them a code – often you both stand to benefit. Best not to pass on their details to firms you've been let down by, though – that sign-up bonus isn't worth losing a friend over. Other big referral scheme firms include gyms and insurers.

The taxman cometh

One quick note on all that extra wonga that you should be seeing flooding into your bank account if you try just some of the above ideas: the taxman will be interested in it too. Everyone can earn up to their personal income allowance without paying tax. Between April 2012 and April 2013, that limit is £8,105 (or £10,500 for those aged sixty-five to seventy-four and £10,660 for those seventy-five and over). If your only income is from mystery shopping, eBay and similar schemes and you don't earn more than that, you don't need to pay tax. But if you're working and are earning more than £8,105 a year, then you'll have to pay tax on your earnings, including any extra money you make, and you may need to register as self-employed. Find out more by contacting your local tax office.

PART 4

Financial stuff

HMM . . . FINANCIAL STUFF. I know this is going to be a struggle. The banks and insurers spend millions using stupid jingles and sexy models trying to make their industries exciting enough to leach some of your cash out of your pocket and into their coffers. All I have is cold, hard type to try to make financial stuff interesting (I hoped for maybe a bit of colour here if my publishers were feeling flush . . . turns out they're on to ausperity too).

But how about this – forget about downgrading your four-ply bog roll to the value, scratchy-bum version; the biggest, and potentially quickest, way to save yourself hundreds – maybe even thousands – of pounds a year, is to take a look at your spending on mortgage repayments, energy bills, credit cards, telecoms and insurance, and switch to a cheaper provider or tariff.

Now I know this is tedious. In fact, having moved house in the midst of writing this book and wedding-planning, even money-saving-nerd me delayed a few months before switching from two different (expensive) gas and electricity providers to one (dual-fuel deals are almost always cheaper). I was busy, it was boring. And it took ages. Because, funnily enough, the energy companies don't take such an interest in *immediately* switching your gas supplier when you request it as they might if you had a late bill payment and they wanted their money. Sometimes, even once you've done the leg work of finding a cheap deal, you end up chasing and chasing and the admin builds up and you wonder, 'Can I be bothered?' But *do* bother! Otherwise, you're just giving in to their money-grabbing ways. And wasting money that you could be spending on having fun.

So here's what I do: I set aside a day, once every six months, and grab my files chock full with hideous bills and tap in my details into comparison sites (read on – these really do make life easy for you), and see if I could save any decent amount that would make switching worthwhile. I do the same a month before my mobile contract and insurance deals run out. Whilst loving the tech world in almost every way, I still prefer to use my paper diary and jot the key dates down each year. If you're more advanced, check out reminder services like tinyurl.com/dealreminder to do this for you.

And because I really, really hate paying more than I have to for intangible things like energy and telecoms (OK, they have tangible benefits, but the provision of energy and a phone line only makes me feel angry if it's not available) my home is also filled with loads of little ways to save. Are you the dad that spends ooh, an hour of your day yelling at the family to switch off the TV/games console/radio/ etc. *properly*? Read on to find out about the standby-killing device that will save your vocal chords by switching off a whole house's electrical devices from one button. And do you have a hippo in your toilet cutting your water bill? No? Get one immediately – they're free from many water companies – to save money and kill the chances of awkward dinner-party silences of the future . . . because you'll soon be waxing lyrical about your water-saving hippo to all and sundry.

If a bill-busting hippo and all-powerful magic button hasn't got you hot and money-savingly excited, well, I tried. But seriously, anyone who hasn't switched energy providers in a decade is practically guaranteed to pocket a hefty annual saving from doing so, whilst taking a gander at phone and other bills every few months saves me at least £50 each time. So tackle each item separately, be methodical and follow the steps below to money-saving success.

If I ever need a final shove, like it's a toss up between watching paint dry and switching car insurance provider, I do some time calculations that go like this: setting aside a couple of boring hours now will save me X pounds on my insurance. I can put the money towards a weekend away next month – and that, I reason, is much more worthwhile than lining the pockets of Mr Moneybags of ExpensiveInsuranceDealsRUs.

Banking

Mortgages

Remortgaging might not be as easy as downgrading your Sainsbury's loo roll to Aldi's version but, with mortgage payments taking the biggest chunk out of earnings for millions of Britons, they are one of the most important components of any financial spring clean.

But despite the fact that switching to a cheaper mortgage is usually homeowners' biggest possible source of monthly savings, a massive two-thirds of Britons are still paying off a mortgage they set up when first moving into their home – even if that was a decade or more ago. If that describes your situation, take some time to look at your options now. With the Bank of England base rate expected to remain at its record low of 0.5 per cent for some years to come, most homeowners who have slipped from fixed-rate or tracker deals arranged at the time of house purchase, on to their lender's standard variable rate (or SVR – the standard interest rate which is set by a particular bank) will make savings by remortgaging.

A small proviso: there are some exceptions. Anyone stuck on an expensive fixed-rate mortgage is likely to face punishing penalties by trying to switch deals. But for most, the monthly savings with a lower interest rate will soon dwarf even early repayment charges.

For anyone considering remortgaging, the two things to find out are the level of equity you currently have in your property, and the rate you are paying right now. To secure the cheapest mortgage rates – for remortgaging or as a first-time buyer – you'll need to own at least a fifteen per cent stake in your home. As for rates, mortgage deals change all the time, but as a rough guide, anyone paying the average bank SVR, which at the time of writing was 4.8 per cent, on a £150,000 mortgage would save a whopping £1,974.98 a year by switching to a two-year tracker mortgage which is presently available at two per cent. Even fixed-rate deals, where you'll be able to know your exact monthly outgoings in advance and protect yourself from future rate rises, are currently available from around three per cent.

You can compare rates yourself via sites like money. co.uk/mortgages.htm, and examine the various costs, fees and interest rates via 'Key Facts' documents: these are laid out in a set format which all mortgage providers have to stick to, making it easier to make comparisons. If, however, you're worried about what's involved in finding the best deal, you may want to seek independent advice. Unbiased. co.uk lists details of independent financial advisors across the UK, which may be helpful. If you do opt to switch independently, remember to compare the full cost, looking out for fees that banks and building societies might impose, such as early repayment charges and arrangement fees.

Credit cards

Whatever the banks claim when shouting about their 'zero per cent interest deals', borrowing money on plastic for anything longer than the normal month always involves some fees or hefty interest, and sometimes both. If possible, avoid it. But because boilers do sometimes explode in the middle of winter and cars do give up the ghost just before that long, crucial drive, it's important to know how, if you do need to go into the red, to do so in the cheapest possible way. That's especially true now: a survey for the Post Office revealed that thirty-six per cent of credit card holders – or some twelve million Britons – are paying for their day-to-day living costs using their cards. Doing so via the cheapest route could easily save hundreds of pounds a year; for large borrowings, it will be even more.

Usually, the cheapest and easiest route to borrowing is via a credit card, but that's only true if your credit score (the number that banks use to rate your creditworthiness, or how likely you are to pay back money – see below) allows you access to the top deals.

Underneath the enormous adverts that banks plaster on billboards and buses to lure you into their latest deals – because credit cards are usually big money-makers for lenders, so they battle amongst themselves to secure customers – will be acres of writing in tiny, tiny fonts about terms and conditions. Obviously it's important to read all this bumph, but, equally obviously, most of us never do so, as we have lives to live. The number to watch out for, then, is the card's APR, or annual percentage rate – how much borrowing money will cost, including interest and charges. Every lender has to provide this number, so it's the easiest way to compare costs and ensure you're paying the lowest possible amount.

The average APR on credit cards in the UK is currently 18.4 per cent, but some are far more. That's why the cheapest way to use a credit card is usually via an interest-free balance transfer or spending deal. These last as long as two years, and mean that over the duration of the zero per cent offer, you pay no interest on the money you owe. That can trigger large savings: someone with a £2,500 debt on a credit card would save around £460 over the course of a year by avoiding the 18.4 per cent interest rate charged on the average plastic. By contrast, anyone with that average credit card would have paid the bank £460 in interest that year, and spent nothing repaying the actual debt.

Remember, though, that APR isn't the only factor: the ultimate cost of borrowing will depend on how quickly or slowly you repay the debt. And whilst interest-free balance transfer offers can help save money, they're not completely free. Most banks demand borrowers pay between two and three per cent of their total debt to shift it across. Still, on a £2,500 debt, the fee would work out at around £65, far less than average interest payments. You'll need to work out whether you'll save more by using the lowest-rate, long-term credit card (usually under ten per cent) or a fixed-term interest-free deal. Moneysavingexpert.com has a feature called 'which card is cheapest' where you can enter your debt and desired monthly repayments, and it will flag up the best deal, without marring your credit rating.

For some, the outlook will be bleaker. With a poor credit rating, banks will either jack up interest rates or point-blank refuse to offer borrowers a credit card. Anyone in that position who still needs to borrow may need to seek out a personal loan, or a lender that specialises in dealing with customers who have been turned down elsewhere. See 'Can't get a credit card?' below.

The borrowing rules

It's crucial to stick to a few rules to make sure your borrowing is as cheap as possible:

1. Boost your chances of acceptance by checking your credit rating and clearing up anything that's dragging it down. See page 235.

2. Pay back at least the minimum repayment. If you don't, you'll lose the interest-free deal and have to pay extra fees.

3. Use any money saved by paying less (or no) interest to pay back the debt. Repaying just over £200 per month on a £2,500 borrowing would clear it in a year. Another reason it's important to pay back as soon as you can is because balance transfer deals won't last forever. Borrowers have been able to take advantage of them recently and roll over debt from one deal to another. But as the wider economy falters, deals may get shorter or start to disappear altogether.

4. You can find the longest balance transfer deal currently available via a banking comparison site such as moneyfacts.co.uk.

5. Watch out for the due-by date. Far more important than a packet of crisps' best-before date, this is when your interest-free deal runs out. Make sure you know when it is, and either pay off your debt in full or switch to a new balance transfer before the end date – otherwise you'll be moved on to a standard credit card deal with a hefty interest rate.

Spending and making money off your credit card

If you pay off your credit card balance in full each month, then use one that rewards you for doing so. Either opt for a cashback card – which pays back a percentage of annual spending each year, so you receive a lump sum in your account – or a credit card with freebies such as travel insurance. Never take out one of these cards if you've got any debts – the interest charges will almost always cost more than the value of any extras – and bear in mind you have to pay off the balance in full each month to reap the rewards. It's best to set up a direct debit from your current account so you don't forget. Make sure you don't go above your borrowing limit – that will trigger punishing fees.

> *'I take out all my disposable income as cash after pay day. That way I know exactly what cash I have to spend on socialising, and other extras, and I don't go overdrawn.'*
> — *CLAIRE, NORTHAMPTON*

For cashback deals, the most generous providers tend to be American Express and Capital One, although high street lenders are dipping a toe into the market too. Look at the various options by using a comparison site (moneysupermarket.com is particularly good on credit cards). Read the small print: some providers will scream about offering five per cent cashback, when in reality that's usually just for the first three months. Most will have a limit on the amount of spending which you can receive cashback from too. Still, stick to the rules and a cashback credit card is an easy way to get something for nothing, particularly if you've got any big purchases lined up. Someone spending £5,000 a year on a card paying out five per cent cashback on up to £2,000-worth of spending for three months, then 1.25 per cent thereafter, would get around £100 back.

But note that cashback providers are increasingly demanding annual fees, usually about £25, so if your annual spending isn't high, make sure you'd earn enough cashback to make the fee back. If not, look at other rewards on offer. Some free credit cards offer discounts on petrol or supermarket spending, or insurance deals. Make the most of 'refer a friend' deals, too. I referred a friend to American Express and we were both given £25: enough for a delicious dinner for two – which we each paid for on the Amex to get cashback.

The credit card guarantee

There's another major benefit to credit cards: all spending on them is covered by the Consumer Credit Act 1974, which makes card providers 'jointly and severally liable' for any breach of contract or misrepresentation by the company. In plain English, what that means is that if you buy something from, say, an online store, and it then doesn't arrive, and the company isn't contactable, or if you order furniture from a shop that goes bust before its delivery, you can claim the money back from the credit card company.

This only comes into play if whatever you've bought costs between £100 and £30,000, but you don't have to have paid for the good(s) in full on your card – the provider is liable even if shoppers put only part of the payment, like a deposit, on plastic, as long as it's between those £100 and £30,000 limits. Note that this guarantee only applies to purchases made on credit, not debit, cards.

If you do find yourself needing to claim this way, consumer group Which? has a useful set of sample letters which you can use as templates for your own claims (see which.co.uk/consumer-rights/sale-of-goods/understanding-the-consumer-credit-act/sample-letters).

Can't get a credit card?

Borrowers whose credit rating means applications for interest-free cards are rejected – or offered at an eye-watering rate – may struggle to find decent rates from other sources. The crucial thing is that you *don't* keep applying to myriad banks in the hope one will accept you. Doing so could just trigger rejection letters – which will do even more damage to your credit rating. Instead, you should first try to improve your credit score – see below – before trying to see if credit cards might then accept you as a result of your work. Do so in a way that won't hit your credit rating, using a so-called 'soft search' via a comparison site. These sites will ask only a few questions, not demand specific personal details, before guiding you to the card most likely to accept you and offer the best rate. Note, though, that if you do go on to apply, acceptance isn't guaranteed. Moneysupermarket.com is amongst the sites which provide soft searches, via its 'smart search' facility.

If no deals are available, any cheap borrowing options will be limited. Examine the costs of authorised overdrafts from banks rather than just going into the red without asking (this will trigger daily fees), or look at rates on offer for personal loans. Make sure you know the difference between secured and unsecured loans. Secured loans mean that the debt is tied to your home or another major asset, and if you don't pay back the loan, the lender can repossess your home and make you homeless. These loans are also at variable rates, so the interest payable can be ramped up by the lender at any point.

Unsecured loans, meanwhile, are usually fixed rate, so you know what your monthly bill will be until you pay the debt back. Although it's not impossible, it's much more difficult for lenders to take hold of assets like your home with an unsecured loan. But personal loans will still be expensive and should be avoided where possible. Seek out debt advice (see the Directory) before plunging further into the red. You may see payday loans advertised, or be approached by firms offering these, but be wary. The Office of Fair Trading is currently investigating this short-term lending industry after complaints about its expensive fees doubled in the past year.

Credit rating

Cleaning up your credit rating is a free, and fast, route to either cutting the cost of securing a credit card, loans or mortgages or boosting your chances of getting one. Credit rating agencies list your repayment history on a vast range of services from mobile phone bills and store cards to credit and debit cards and loans, as well as other information including past addresses, and use it all to give you a credit score. It's this that lenders use to decide whether to accept you as a customer, and, if so, what rate to offer. So the worse your credit rating, the less likely you are to secure a good deal.

But agencies make mistakes, and spending some time seeking out your record and fixing any errors or adding notes to explain (relevant) reasons for any delayed payments may bring down the cost of borrowing considerably. So check your credit report by signing up with an agency like Experian (experian.co.uk) or Equifax (equifax.co.uk) for a free trial. Do so via a cashback site (see page 19) and you'll normally receive some money for joining, so will actually end up getting paid to view your report – but make sure you remember to cancel your trial afterwards to avoid being billed a monthly fee. Once you've signed up and provided some basic information such as your address and current account provider, your credit report will be available a few minutes later.

Read through it to check for any 'black marks' like missed payments. If any are listed that didn't actually take place, contact the credit agency with proof such as bank statements covering the relevant period. If there are marks that did actually happen, but were caused by extraordinary events, add notes to say so. For example, if serious illness led to missed credit card payments, contact the agency with a doctor's note or other proof and ask for a 'notice of correction' to be added to the information on your record.

There's also more general housekeeping you can do to boost your credit rating in the long term. Close any unused bank accounts, mobile phone contracts or store cards, get on the electoral role or have proof of residency in the UK, install a landline telephone, and always make your repayment schedule. If you do mess up and fall into trouble, contact your lender to ask for help. They may agree to organise a smaller minimum monthly payment or have other suggestions. Being proactive will help you to both avoid penalties and stop damaging your credit record for the future.

Savings

If and when all the penny-pinching and money-making ideas in this book leave you a little extra to put aside into a nest egg, you'll want it to work hard for you, and grow. Unfortunately in the current climate that's not easy. The record low Bank of England interest rate means the banks are offering stingy interest rates themselves: the average savings account pays out less than 0.5 per cent. When you take into account inflation, any savings will actually end up being eroded in value. But before you go and blow those savings on a stash of champers instead, shop around. The market leading instant-access savings account tends to pay out over three per cent, and if you're willing and able to lock away your money for longer you can secure far more interest. Find the current top-paying savings account at moneynet.co.uk. If you can, it's a good idea to set up a regular savings plan, putting away as much as you can each month. Doing so can trigger more generous interest rates, sometimes as high as seven per cent.

All taxpayers will see their savings eroded by tax unless they invest via a tax-efficient scheme such as an ISA. These help savers avoid giving more of their money than necessary to the taxman. Normally, every £1 of interest earned in a savings account is taxed at twenty per cent, leaving you, as a saver, with only 80p. If you're a higher-rate or top-rate taxpayer, you'll receive as little as 50p in interest, after tax. But put the money into a cash ISA, and you are able to keep all the interest. This year you can put up to £5,640 in a cash ISA account, and either the same again invested in an investment stocks and shares ISA, or the whole £11,280 in an investment ISA. If you don't use your annual allowance in one tax year, it disappears forever.

Oh, and if you win the lottery, successfully sue your pillow for giving you neck ache or come into a large stash of cash in some other way, remember to spread your funds around. The government will guarantee the first £85,000 of your savings in one registered bank or building society under the Financial Services Compensation Scheme. But if you have more than that, share your cash between several registered institutions to avoid losing out if a bank goes bust. Check which institutions are included at fscs.org.uk or call 0800 678 1100.

Retirement

It might seem ages away, or it might be just around the corner. But if you want to be able to afford a decent retirement, it's crucial to start planning as early as you can. Who knows what the state will be able to afford to provide for your twilight years in a decade or two to come. So if your workplace runs a pension scheme that has free or matching contributions, bite off your boss's arm to join it. Each year you can put £2,880 into a pension, and then the government adds £720, making a total of £3,600 squirreled away for the future, plus you avoid paying tax on your annual contributions.

From 2018, all UK employees aged between twenty-two and the state pension age, and earning at least £8,105 a year, will be automatically enrolled in a pension scheme with employer contributions. But until then, if your workplace doesn't offer this or you are not working, you might want to consider a personal pension, usually bought from pension companies, insurers, banks or building societies.

Compensation

If you don't ask, you don't get. And if you don't complain about bad service or products, it won't get any better for other people – and you won't get anything back. Don't overlook the value of a good whinging session. I always complain to big businesses at any sign of bad service, and it usually triggers some kind of refund or vouchers. In the past I've contacted my mobile phone provider about dropped calls and been given a month's free line rental, had a late-payment fee from my bank returned because I pointed out it was the first time I'd erred . . . and been given a £5 voucher from Pret A Manger because my duck wrap contained too much hoisin sauce, so it dripped on my jacket. Sure, some might say I should have taken care where to apply my gob . . . But I like to hope that in the future, Pret won't over-sauce its sarnies. And I scored a free lunch.

If you receive bad service or a faulty good and complain, it's also worth asking companies if they will also pay compensation for your time. If you've spent ten minutes or so on the phone waiting to moan about something that's gone wrong, a lot of firms will offer around a fiver in compensation.

And whilst it's always worth having a moan about life's little irritations, whether they are sandwiches or late trains (see page 192), it's really, really worth complaining when it comes to dodgy service or sales in financial services.

PPI IOU?

The recent scandal over mis-sold payment protection insurance, or PPI – an add-on product guarding against missed repayments on loans, credit cards and mortgages in the event of accident, illness or unemployment – broke after thousands of customer complaints. Eventually the industry watchdog, the Financial Services

Authority, introduced rules to stop mis-selling, including making it clear cover is optional, and forced banks to pay out compensation. But there are still millions more cases out there, so it's worth taking a few minutes to think about whether yours could be one of them. Salesmen have been flogging PPI on products ranging from personal loans and credit card accounts to mortgages over the past decade or so.

If you were not told that PPI insurance was optional at the point of purchase, you're likely to have a case. Likewise, the vendor must have told you about major exclusions to the policy, like pre-existing medical problems, and have advised that it would have to have been paid for at the point of purchase. Most PPI insurance policies last only five years, so if your loan or finance agreement lasted longer than that, the seller should have made it clear that the insurance would run out before the end of the loan term. He or she must also have made it clear that, even after the policy ran out, you would continue to pay interest on the insurance premium. If any of these aspects were not explained to you when you bought a PPI policy, then you may well have a case. Now, what to do about it . . .

Dig out your paperwork, and carry out the claim yourself, because any winning case will then be far more lucrative. You can't watch any daytime TV without being bombarded by 'no win, no fee' PPI claims firms begging you to 'give them a call' – but they will take a cut of any compensation, perhaps taking as much as a third, and using them doesn't make it any more likely that you'll win.

Plus, complaining on your own isn't difficult. The first step is to approach your bank or financial services provider with your case and paperwork. Consumer group Which? has an easy tool on its website to take you through each stage, and it even generates a complaint letter on your behalf.

The bank or financial services provider should respond to you within eight weeks. If they don't, the next step is to take your complaint to the Financial Ombudsman Service (financial-ombudsman.org. uk). Almost nine out of ten Britons who took their PPI complaint to the FOS's service (which is free) last year received a decision in their favour. If you are awarded compensation, but are forced to wait an unreasonable time to receive it, you may be awarded extra money. The FOS demands banks must pay any interest due on compensation up to the point of payment, so if yours has been delayed, make a second claim for that extra cash.

Telecoms

If you've had the same BT phone line and deal in your home since Maureen Lipman played Beattie Bellman in its adverts, I'll bet my surgically attached mobile that you'll be able to save money on your phone bill by switching. Cheap providers have stormed into the market and, even though you'll still have to pay the standard monthly line rental, you can still find phone deals for less than £10 a month. That's if you don't like to chat much. And even if you do, packages with inclusive minutes and free talking times are available for not much more.

If you're willing to switch home phone providers, the golden rule is to shop around. (And, in fact, even if you can't be bothered to go through with it, it's still worth doing this research as you can then go back to your current provider, tell them you've been offered a deal, and watch them drop your rate.)

Look beyond the dominant players like BT and Virgin Media: over the past year, for example, the Post Office and Primus have been consistently amongst the cheapest providers. Primus' home rental saver at £8.99 a month includes free evening and weekend calls to UK landlines. By contrast, the standard line rental for BT costs £14.60, again with evening calls to home phones in Britain included. Pay a visit to comparison site homephonechoices.co.uk, which lists the best unlimited weekend calls or anytime call packages. But before signing up to a new deal, remember to clear your computer's cookies or use another computer to do the actual joining process, because if you buy your new package via a cashback website (see page 19) you'll receive as much as £100 for switching home phone providers.

Other home phone deals are available if you've got – or want to get – broadband or satellite TV installed at home. Seek out the cheapest bundles at simplifydigital.co.uk – a site backed by the government's industry regulator Ofcom (see below for more info). But note that if you're buying a bundle, it's usually worth trying to speak to a sales representative before signing up: since telecoms is highly competitive, providers will trip over themselves to sign you up with top deals. Just make sure you move on when the offer period comes to an end.

But back to home phone lines. If you don't want to switch providers, or already have, there are still lots of ways to save:

- Switch to pay via direct debit: as an example, BT customers save £22 a year by switching.

- Only make long, chatty calls (or, if you're feeling stingy, all calls) during off-peak times. For BT and TalkTalk, peak calling periods are 7 a.m. – 7 p.m., whilst at Virgin Media and the Post Office it's 6 a.m. – 6 p.m., and Primus is 8 a.m. – 6 p.m.

- Hang up after an hour's nattering: although providers describe call packages as 'unlimited', that's usually not true. They tend to be free only for the first sixty minutes, so keep an eye on the time, and if it's approaching an hour, end the call and redial.

- Consider paying a year's worth of line rental up front. BT's option to do so – called Line Rental Saver – costs £120 for the year, saving £55.20 a year compared to paying monthly. But if you do so, make sure you're convinced by the company's solvency: if it was to go bust during the year, you'd most likely lose your upfront payment.

- Never just pick up the phone and dial premium numbers. Instead, find alternatives to 0871 and other expensive phone numbers by visiting saynoto0870. com. Just tap the number or the company name into the site and it will bring up a low-cost or Freephone alternative to many.

- Follow the same rule if you're phoning abroad: never dial the number of Uncle Harry in Hyderabad – instead, search for a cheap prefix to slash the cost. There are hundreds of providers who do this, but each charges a different amount for calling different locations. So use a comparison site: select the country you want to phone at niftylist.co.uk/calls, input whether you're dialling from a land line or mobile, and it will flag up a list of the cheapest providers. Phoning an Indian landline direct from a BT phone would cost 22p per minute during the daytime, but call instead with the cheapest override telecoms provider that you find on Niftylist or elsewhere and you will pay only 0.51p per minute. Which is a lot more Harry for your money.

- The last rule of phone cost-cutting is: don't buy more than you are using. If you tend to be out during most of the weekend, don't bother paying extra for unlimited weekend calls. And minimise use of your home phone for outgoing calls. One easy way is to use the inclusive minutes on your mobile contract, if applicable, to make calls. Another is to sign up to a free online telephony site to chat. On Skype, VBuzzer or Google Voice, for example, users can talk direct to others with the same software for free. Many also offer cheap deals to call landlines in the UK and overseas, plus apps where you can download the software to your mobile and use that to contact others with the same programmes on their phones or computers for free.

'Pay by direct debit. You will usually save money by paying this way and it will mean you won't end up making late payments and incurring fines.'
— *SHAZIA, SURREY*

Mobiles

One major area of money-wasting that always shocks me is how much people spend on their mobiles each month. So many of my friends have happily signed up to £30 or even £40 a month mobile contracts because, at the end of their existing deal, their operator offered them a snazzy new phone and 'all you have to do is agree to stay with us for another two years.' But that monthly £30 bill – and that's without slipping into extra usage or venturing abroad – tots up to £360 a year. And some mobile contracts are harder to get out of than marriages.

So next time your contract is ending, remember this: it's likely that you'll be able to secure your same number of monthly minutes, texts and/or data for a lower price by taking some simple action. Sadly, it's tough to do this if you're in the middle of a contract. The exit fee will likely be so large it would dwarf any potential savings. But if you're on a pay-as-you go deal, or coming to the end of a contract, read on.

Research by billmonitor.com found three quarters of phone users waste £200 a year by being on the wrong contract. The website analysed 28,000 phone bills and found most users are chucking away money by paying for far more minutes, data, or text messages than they actually use. The way to get around this is to look at your bills over the past few months and work out exactly how much you're using. But there's a lazy way to do this: tap your phone number into billmonitor.com, omio.com or moneysupermarket.com. The sites will calculate how many monthly minutes, texts and, if you have a smartphone, data you're using, and highlight the cheapest tariffs on a range of networks.

Now, to secure a new deal. If you use your phone infrequently, a pay-as-you go deal will probably work out cheapest. Or if you are happy with your current mobile handset and don't want to upgrade to a new one, opt for a sim-only deal to avoid paying for a phone you don't need. The only caveat is that it can be lucrative to agree to a new handset, which means you could then sell on your old one (see page 210). Look at potential sales values before deciding whether this is worth the hassle.

Once you know what your mobile usage demands are, visit onecompare.com, where you can look for tariffs either by phone, manufacturer or mobile usage. (Quick saving idea for smartphone users: keep your Wi-Fi switched on so your phone automatically connects to free wireless hubs that are now all over the country, including libraries, restaurants and even shops like John Lewis. Doing so will help keep your data usage down.)

'Get rid of your landline and only have a mobile – no one uses their landline anyway and most mobile contracts come with deals that make it free to call other mobiles, which landlines don't provide.' – JOE, LONDON

You'll need to be careful with some of the tariffs on offer. Some sites offer free gifts such as games consoles or 'redemption' cashback offers, where users have to send in bills on specific dates to receive money back. But these can be unreliable. I signed up to one a few years ago, buying an Orange contract via a mobile website who promised me £300 cashback over the two-year contract if I complied with their paperwork. I had to send in bills every three months and they had to arrive within a very short window of time. I used recorded delivery to avoid being a victim of postal problems and wrote the key dates in my diary in red, but I still accidentally missed one deadline – and the company then said I wouldn't be able to reclaim any future payments because I'd strayed from the terms and conditions. Ouch.

Others have reported signing up to these deals and finding the go-between firm later went bust, leaving them with a contract with the mobile company but no opportunity for cashback.

So these may be best avoided unless you use a source that you know to be both reputable and financially strong. You can, though, secure cashback for buying new mobile deals in the usual way through the likes of Topcashback or Quidco (see page 19) but even here, remember payment isn't guaranteed until it actually arrives in your bank account, so ensure you can afford the contract without it.

Once you have found your top deal, this is where the game-playing strategy comes in. You have worked out what you could be paying for what you want: you have found your ultimate deal. But you want to avoid the hassle of swapping. Imagine Fred has found a £25 contract with Four Mobile with 400 minutes, unlimited texts, a data bundle and the BlackBerry that he wants. Fred is currently paying £40 a month on Banana Mobile, and his contract is coming to an end. But he has been with Banana for the past decade. He knows he can get a good signal at his home and at work, and he can't be bothered with the hassle of switching.

All he has to do is phone Banana's customer services. The person who answers the phone will try to get Fred to stick with Banana. He might offer a package for £30. But Fred still says no. 'The deal isn't as good as one I've been offered by Four, which offers the same package for £25,' he tells the Banana salesman. As a result, Fred will be transferred to a separate area of the call centre, with near-magical deal power: it's called the 'retentions' department. In a bid to keep ten-year-loyal Fred as a Banana customer, the retentions salesperson agrees to match the Four deal.

And that's it. Four easy steps to secure a cheaper mobile contract:

1. Find out what you're using
2. Source the best offer
3. See if your current operator will match it
4. Or switch

If you go through with a switch, make sure your signal strength is good enough throughout your home, work, or wherever you use your mobile most. The telecoms providers all have coverage maps on their websites. And remember, if you get a new handset, recycling the old one could leave you as much as £200 richer. See page 210.

'Make the most of the hundreds of online freebies. You won't have to pay to get photos developed (or at least will only pay postage) if you sign up to a different site's 'free deals for new customers' offer every time you need photos. Snapfish, Photobox and Truprint all offer these. Other websites offer free food, drink and cosmetics samples, free plant seeds, books and more. Keep an eye on an aggregator site like magicfreebies.co.uk or money.co.uk to stay up to date on the freebies.' – DIANA, OXFORD

Paid TV

A year ago I was invited on to a Sky News TV show to talk about money saving. The presenter asked me for my top money-saving tips, and I responded that the first thing to do when household spending needed to be cut back was trim the extras – like gym membership and Sky TV subscription. The Sky presenter's face froze in shock, as I laughed, nervously. It's true, though: over the course of a year, paid-for TV packages really do mount up. Never think about the monthly, say £30, cost of a contract, but the reality of what you're paying each year, and whether you'd prefer to spend that £360 on a week of sunshine abroad, say, or forty trips to the cinema to see the films you're paying to see on TV, on the big screen.

If the answer is no, and you're a massive sports fan or movie buff who does want to take out or keep up a TV subscription, don't pay over the odds for it. Work out what channels you actually want and, if you're a newcomer, research for the best deals online using simplifydigital. co.uk/digital-tv. Before buying, again remember to use a cashback site (see page 19) to sign up, as new TV contracts will be rewarded with up to £150.

If you're already a customer of Sky, Virgin Media or another provider and want to stick with them, it's still worth carrying out a bit of research to cut your bill. Providers are usually uber-keen to keep customers on board, so as your contract nears its close, phone your provider and say you've found a cheaper deal elsewhere (that's where the research kicks in: they'll want to know the details, so you use the above method to track down a better offer for the salesperson to match). Tell the salesperson that, well, you don't want to leave, but with the better deal in the offing . . . If they don't budge on your renewal price, say you'd like to end the contract. This will usually see your call passed on to someone senior in the 'customer retentions' team, who have more deals firepower. If not, you can always backtrack, say you'll think about it, and try to speak to someone more sympathetic on another day.

Energy

We're paying more than ever before for energy bills. Some sombre statistics: our cumulative spending on energy is nearly £2 billion each year, the average family's bill has doubled over the past six years – and the carbon-cutting targets mean that bills are set to rise even more over the next few years. And that's why I'm sitting here in three jumpers, shivering, and trying to put off turning on the heating. More price rises are going to be painful, especially considering the average household's energy bill is already over £1,200 a year, and fuel poverty – where people can't afford their energy bills – is set to affect 8.5 million Britons by 2016.

That's why it's important to save in any way possible. Those who will be able to make the biggest savings are those who are on old, non-internet tariffs, paying separate firms for gas and electricity. Yet according to figures from the government energy watchdog, Ofgem, fifty-eight per cent of gas customers and fifty-seven per cent of electricity customers have never switched supplier. As I said, until recently, I was one of them. It felt like a whole lot of hassle to work out the latest meter reading, spend yonks on the phone to various unhelpful energy companies, and change direct debits – just the thought of it made me write 'switch energy' on my to-do list, and never get around to it. I figured all suppliers were pretty much the same, and I'd just painfully swallow the enormous bill four times a year. But after prices rose yet again, I made myself take action. And it's worth it. Consumers who have never before switched supplier – or haven't done so for years – save an average of twenty-two per cent by moving to the cheapest provider, according to figures from MoneySupermarket. On top of that, you can rack up as much as £100 cashback by switching to some providers, and if you're feeling lazy, it's even possible to get someone to do the legwork for you, without paying a penny. Here's how:

1. First, make sure you're not tied into a deal. This is only likely if you've signed a new contract in the last eighteen months, but it's worth checking, as otherwise you could face penalties.

2. Next, you'll need to check if it is possible to get a better deal. To do so, you'll need to have your accurate energy usage to hand, including the name of your current supplier, the tariff you're on, and how much energy you consume, either in kilowatt hours (kWh) or as a monthly or quarterly spend. You'll find all this info laid out clearly on your last bill.

3. Enter this information into a comparison service. Online, energyhelpline.com is comprehensive and offers up to £30 cashback. It also has a phone line – 0800 074 0745 – for those who are not online. Other sites include uswitch.com, which has a postal service alongside its online offering: just send in your bill, and an adviser will phone back to tell you about your options.

4. When switching, you will face several options. Dual-fuel tariff or separate gas and electricity providers? You

should check, but generally, dual fuel is cheaper. How to pay? Monthly direct debit is usually cheapest, since providers cut rates by around ten per cent for those who pay in this way. But you'll need to ensure you have the cash ready in the account each month.

5. Don't necessarily stick to the big players. The energy you receive – and how it gets into your home – will be exactly the same, whoever you opt for; the only difference is price and customer service. Smaller, newer companies like First Utility, OVO Energy and Co-operative Energy are trying to boost their share of the market and so may have better deals.

6. If you expect energy costs to rise, or find it helpful to allocate an exact amount each month for gas and electricity to help your budget, look up fixed-price deals and see how the price differs. Sometimes they are a lot more expensive, but not always, and they enable you to plan ahead on spending.

7. Once you've found the cheapest deal, visit a cashback site to see if the cheapest provider is giving away any incentives. I received £70 for switching dual-fuel providers last year – which helped towards the winter energy bills. Remember to clear your cookies (see page 20) before clicking the link from a cashback site to ensure you receive your payments.

8. Once you've organised the switch, the new energy provider will do the rest for you, but it's worth taking a reading of your meter on changeover day, to make sure you're not overcharged by either your new or old provider. Often you'll be asked to send in a meter

reading anyway. Switching usually takes between four and six weeks.

9. Continue doing meter readings every time you receive a bill from your provider – estimates are often far too high so you'll be wasting money, and if they're too low, you'll be whacked with a whopping bill at the end of the year, which is best avoided too.

There's another, lazier way. Incahoot.com, a group-discount site, offers its own deals on energy bills and has a 'concierge' service to help those who can't be bothered to switch energy provider – just send a copy of your latest bill to the site and it will work out how much money it is possible to save, then contact your old supplier and set up a direct debit to a new one on your behalf. The money saved might not add up to the same amount as the above route, because you could miss out on a cashback bonus, but Incahoot will even contact your old providers and fill in all the forms for you (although you obviously have to give your permission and sign the final papers) so it's a money-saver for those with little time.

Energy-saving ideas

Once you've switched to the cheapest supplier, there's nothing else you can do to control the price per unit of your energy, but you can cut bills by using less of the stuff. Doing so is also greener. Sometimes you'll have to shell out a bit at first, but usually the costs are quickly wiped out by the savings.

At its most basic, the way to cut energy bills is simply to use less of it. So instead of switching on the heating in October, wear extra jumpers for a few weeks and wait till it's much colder in November. If you need more of an incentive, some claim being cold makes your body work harder and aids weight loss. If your central heating is on a timer, set it to come on fifteen minutes later and go off fifteen minutes earlier – doing so every day will save forty-two hours' worth of energy usage in the three coldest months of winter. Put your hot water gauge's temperature down a notch – or a bit more if you've got a teenager that you want to shock out of the shower they've been standing in for thirty minutes. Hot water cylinder thermostats don't need to be set higher than 60°C or 140°F.

Stop wasting energy by preventing heat loss. If you haven't already got it, install loft and cavity wall insulation to stop heat escaping from the roof and walls – doing so can save as much as £650 a year on fuel bills. Loft insulation will cost between £50 and £300, depending on the size of your loft and whether you do it yourself or call in the professionals. But experts reckon it only takes two years to pay for itself, because stopping most of the heat loss through the roof will save the average household as much as £200 a year. The Big Six energy providers sometimes offer free insulation as part of their agreement with the government to cut Britain's carbon dioxide emissions, so check with your provider (or just look around you: they're often so proud of their good deed that it's advertised on every billboard going).

Unless you're on benefits, you'll usually have to pay extra for the insulation to be installed, even if it is free or subsidised. But if your loft is easy to move around in and you're fit and nimble, it's not difficult to do it yourself: just buy rolls of mineral wool insulation. You'll need to lift any floorboards first, if you have them, but use boarding to stand on rather than the loft's joists (the beams that make up its flooring), because most are not load-bearing. Start from the eaves and work towards the centre of your loft, each time layering around the joists, then add a second layer running at ninety degrees from the first to cover the joists and double the insulation's depth. Then re-board the loft.

It's also worth investigating wall insulation. This is best left to the experts so, to find out more and for help if you're not able or keen to install loft insulation yourself, check out the list of registered installers at nationalinsulationassociation. org.uk.

If your boiler is getting on a bit, one of the best ways to boost a home's efficiency is to replace it. Boilers make up about two-thirds of annual spending on energy, and the Energy Saving Trust reports that switching from a G-rated boiler to an A-rated condensing boiler could save as much as £300 a year, as well as cutting your home's carbon emissions. That's the good news. The bad news? New boilers are expensive: on average, about £2,500 including installation. There are, however, lots of discounts and grants available depending on your household circumstances and location. See est.org.uk/take-action to find out what you could be entitled to. If you decide to go ahead and buy a new boiler, the Energy Saving Trust's advice centre (0300 123 1234 in England, Wales and Northern Ireland or 0800 512 012 in Scotland) can offer help finding a registered installer, or see centralheating.co.uk. Follow the usual rules for building work (see page 161) to avoid getting ripped off.

Close off any draughts using draught excluders under

doors and flaps behind letterboxes, key holes or cat flaps. Stick draught-proofing strips around windy window frames to fill any gaps. On doors, cover up keyholes with a hinged metal circle that can be bought for a pound from a DIY store, and install a letterbox flap or brush. You can buy a device like an ecoflap (ecoflap.co.uk) to stops chilly winds coming through your letterbox, but it costs around £20 so you may want to try to make your own. Cracks or gaps in draughty floorboards, walls or skirting boards should be filled using a filler product.

'Instead of using the tumble drier, drape clothes around the house on banisters, chairs, hangers, radiators and clothes horses – it looks messy but they don't take long too dry. My grandkids often use them as them as tents too, so it doubles up as cheap entertainment.' – LYN, BOURNEMOUTH

Stick silver radiator foil to the walls behind house radiators – they will reflect heat away from the walls and back into your home. Or you can buy specially made metallised PVC panels that fit neatly – and unseen – behind your radiator and save up to twenty per cent on energy bills. The cost of a pack of twenty Heatsaver radiator panels – enough to fit the average three-bedroom semi – is £50.55, and the makers claim they cut energy bills by a fifth, saving the average homeowner £146 a year.

Other energy-savers worth splashing out on include a canny-looking device called a chimney balloon (there's one example at chimneyballoon.co.uk but they are available in major DIY stores too) which stops warm air exiting homes and cold air coming in through chimneys. But remember to remove it if you have a working fireplace and are planning to light up. Water-tank jackets also stem energy losses: a British Standard jacket can cost as little as £10, but cuts heat loss by over three quarters – warmer than your average anorak. If it's at least 75mm thick, it will save households as much as £40 each year, so the initial cost will pay for itself within three months. Another warmer that will pay dividends is pipe insulation, which wraps around exposed hot water pipes to slash heat loss. It's easy to install: see energysavingtrust.org.uk.

Electricity

Thinking twice about how you use appliances saves money and effort. For example, that short wash you put on the other day just so you could wear the cream top with the ketchup stain? Shouldn't have bothered. The cost of using a washing machine depends on the water used and temperature set, and on a short wash, you'll still need the water to get to the required temperature, but it will have to do so more quickly. You'll end up doing more washing too.

Instead, wait till your basket is full before putting on a wash, and don't go crazy with detergent: putting more in doesn't mean a cleaner load. For not-that-dirty washing, consider switching to a 30°C cycle: doing so regularly will knock about £10 a year off energy costs. The same is true for dishwashers: half loads don't use half the amount of energy and water as full ones. Likewise, if any appliance has an 'eco' setting, use it to save resources and money. When buying new appliances, opting for the most efficient models will usually work out cheaper in the long-run, even though the initial outlay may be more. (See page 40 on buying household appliances.)

Fridges and freezers run most efficiently when they are at least three-quarters full. Avoid standing in front of them gazing (or grazing) for too long: it will then need to use more energy to get back to its pre-set temperature. Unless you're in a hurry, stick frozen food in the fridge to defrost – it will cool down the rest of your fridge food too. Elsewhere in the kitchen, don't overfill the kettle, only pour in as much water as you need for that cuppa or saucepan.

Now it's time to look up. Light bulbs make up about ten per cent of the average electricity bill, so switching to low-energy bulbs can trigger big savings. Whilst traditional bulbs are at least forty watts, their eco alternatives can be as little as eight watts. Although they're more expensive at first, they last as long as ten years, so cost less in the long term. You won't have to get on that wobbly ladder so many times either. According to the Energy Saving Trust, fitting one eco-friendly light bulb like a compact fluorescent or LED bulb will save an average of £3 each year, so swapping all the inefficient bulbs in your home for energy-saving alternatives will save households as much as £55 per year.

Even with eco light bulbs, never forget that golden rule your dad was always shouting about: *Turn off the lights*. It's a myth that you'll waste more energy by switching a bulb on and off – even if you're only going out of a room for a few seconds, it'll still be greener, and cheaper, to switch off the lights. For outside garden or security lights, save money by fitting a motion sensor that switches them on when someone walks past rather than leaving them glaring all night. If you're worried about the wandering alley cats strolling past your door and wasting energy, fit a time switch too – if you're always in by midnight, for example, the light could be programmed not to go on between midnight and whenever it gets dark the following day.

In the rest of the house, your biggest energy-suckers are probably your gadgets on standby. All those TVs, DVD players, laptops, hi-fis and more are using electricity – if only a little – whilst not being used. So instead of putting them on standby, turn them off. If you or others in the house are constantly leaving their computers on standby, it might be worth investing £10 in an ecobutton. When the button is pushed, it instantly puts appliances into hibernation mode (eco-button.com). Or to zap the whole house's on-standby equipment off easily, a device like Standby Buster, which costs around £15, might be worthwhile. It comes with a collection of plugs that you insert into key devices, and a remote control which can be used to zap any electrical appliances on standby around the house.

But switch off anything you're not using from the plug – printers, routers and broadband modems tend to be left ready to spring into action at any moment, but usually power up faster than computers so there's no need for them to be on all the time. Switch off unused phone chargers left clinging to wall plugs. And using wind-up torches and radios, plus rechargeable batteries, will cut the seemingly endless need for Duracells.

Water

The average person in England and Wales uses 150 litres of water a day – which is the equivalent of a milkman delivering 264 pints to your doorstep. The majority is used for washing and flushing the loo, but there's also drinking, cooking, washing the car and watering the garden to think of. Power showers and thirsty household appliances mean we're wasting almost fifty per cent more water than we did twenty-five years ago, according to the Environment Agency. It's not very green, or economical, so what to do about it?

Well, first let's think about your bill and make sure you're not paying for more than you're using. Unlike energy, you can't switch water suppliers, but if your household has more bedrooms than people living in it, try switching to a metered water bill. Comparison site uSwitch found the average unmetered bill came in at £361 last year, whilst the average metered bill was £305. The Consumer Council for Water has a calculator to help work out if you'd save money with a meter at ccwater.org.uk. If the answer is yes, just ask your water provider to install it – they'll do so for free.

Now, on to cutting your bill by slashing your sloshing. First, make sure you haven't got any leaks, and replace worn washers on any leaky taps. Turn off the tap when you're not using it – so don't leave it gushing whilst brushing your teeth, and fill a bowl for washing-up rather than rinsing individual items under the running tap. Choose showers over baths: the average eight-minute shower uses 62 litres of hot water (although some power showers can use up to 136 litres), whilst a bath uses 80 litres. Switch to a water-efficient shower head and you'll use more like 32 litres.

If you're in need of a new loo, opt for a low-flush or dual flush model (you know, the ones with the 'wee' button and the 'both' button). These use as much as six litres less water per flush than traditional toilets. You can also install a dual-flush insert device into your existing loo, or seek out some flush-saving bags or Hippo water-savers – a £3 box that sits in the loo's cistern and promises to save between one and three litres of water per flush, saving about £25 worth of water per year for the average home. Some water companies give out water-saving devices for free, so enquire if yours is one of them.

'Invest in thick socks and a big jumper to save on heating – I speak from experience. My husband is so concerned about energy bills that I wear two pairs of socks and a thick cardie around the house almost every day of winter!'
— SARAH, LEEDS

In the garden, buy a water butt to collect rain water, and use it, rather than a hosepipe, to drench plants if it hasn't rained. Again some water companies provide these for free or at a discount, so check before getting your wallet out. Be wary of water sprinklers: they can use as much water in an hour as a family of four do all a day. Do your watering in the evening or early morning to prevent it evaporating off into the sunshine, and consider topping your flower beds with bark or pebbles, which lock in moisture. Always wash your car with a bucket and sponge rather than a hosepipe.

How much does it cost? (Figures from uSwitch)

Activity	Average weekly use	Litres used – per activity	Cost per use
Bath	2	80 per bath	15p
Flushing the toilet	35	8 per flush	1.52p
Gravity shower	7	35 per shower	7p
Power shower	7	80 per shower	15p
Washing machine	3	65 per wash	12p
Dishwasher	4	25 per wash	5p
Watering the garden	1	540	£1.03
Washing car with bucket	1 (4 buckets)	8 per bucket = 32 litres	6p
Washing car with hosepipe	1	400–480	76p–91.2p

Insurance

Is there anything less fun to buy than insurance? We buy it either because we have to (car insurance, building cover), or we're too scared of the consequences if we don't (life insurance, health policies) – but we always buy it hoping very hard that we never have to use it. And if we do have to claim, the premiums just get more expensive the following year.

Then, even when we don't go within a hundred miles of our insurance policy all year long, the price still goes up anyway. The average car insurance policy rose by fifteen per cent to £971 in 2011, while home insurance cover costs increased by six per cent to beyond £200, according to the AA's premium index. But there are a host of ways to slash the cost of buying a policy. Some are the insurance industry's biggest secrets – the little ways they push up quotes via over-insurance or unnecessary extras in the hope the rest of us won't notice – and some are just clever ways to buy the same policy for less. Here they are, laid out to help you cut the cost of your insurance quote, whatever it is for.

All insurance policies

The golden rule is this: never, ever accept your renewal price. Ever. It's *always* possible to make it cheaper by either finding another provider, or, if you can't be bothered to do that, simply phoning up and threatening to cancel the policy because you've found an equivalent one that costs less – they'll lower the price to keep your business.

Rule number two is to visit a comparison site – or a few if you've got a bit more time, as they don't all cover every provider – and tap in your details. Just searching the market in this way triggers an average saving of £370. Using moneysupermarket.com, confused.com and gocompare. com will cover the vast majority of the market. However, for some areas of insurance, particularly car and home, you may reach a better deal by going direct: more details below.

'*Make sure you review your insurance's small print. I've found myself buying aspects that I don't need and later found what's covered wasn't what I'd expected because I didn't get round to reading the details.*'

– *LAURENCE, LEEDS*

Once you've found the best deal that matches your needs (and go through the policy with a nit-picking comb to see that it both covers exactly what you want and strips out extras you don't need – comparison sites may mask the terms and conditions; see below) it's time to buy. Never buy just by clicking on the link from the comparison site. Doing so triggers a payback from the insurer to the shop-around site. That's not a problem in itself, but you could be snaffling up that kick-back if you use a cashback site, and insurance policies are amongst the most generous cashback products and help provide a serious saving on your overall insurance cost.

Some other general tips to shave more from insurance costs: buy cover in full rather than via monthly payments, as it works out cheaper that way. If you can't afford to shell out for the full amount, check whether you could afford to do so via an interest-free credit card. As long as you repay the balance before the end of the deal's term, it will be cheaper than on monthly payments to an insurer. And try to find quotes well before renewal time: major insurers including Barclays, Aviva, Churchill and Direct Line all remain valid for three months, and when prices are rising, you may secure a cheaper deal by setting the price well before the policy begins.

Car insurance

There are three levels of cover: third party insures against damage and injuries that you, or your passenger, cause to someone else or their property in a car accident, but it doesn't pay out in the event of any damage to you or your car. Third party, fire and theft covers the above as well as providing insurance if your vehicle is stolen or burnt by fire. And comprehensive car insurance extends that to cover any damage to your own car too.

Logic might suggest third-party policies, which include the least cover, would be priced the lowest. But nowadays that's rarely true. Since insurers reckon someone applying for third-party cover might not be the most responsible driver, for most people – especially those with a year or more no-claims discount (NCD) – quotes for comprehensive cover will come out cheaper.

After that, the next aspect of your policy most likely to affect price (apart from your vehicle and where you live, which you're probably not going to change for the sake of your car insurance policy) is the NCD. Companies offer wildly varying discounts for these: Which? reports one year's claim-free motoring can trigger a discount of as much as fifty-eight per cent or as little as twenty-seven per cent, depending on the insurer. Usually the maximum no-claims discount is around seventy per cent for four years' driving without making a claim. For new drivers and those who are having to rebuild an NCD after a crash, there is a way to accelerate your years of discount without travelling through time: opt for a ten-month policy. These are available from a host of insurers, including elephant. co.uk and Admiral, and can be a useful way to build up or rebuild an NCD.

One of the easiest ways to save on car insurance is to add a friend or relative who is a lower-risk driver to your policy. Never add them as the main, named driver – that's called fronting, and is illegal. But, even if the person in question is not going to drive your car, adding them as an extra driver will often bring down the cost. Popping my dad on to my policy drops the price of my quote by a full £100. Thanks, Dad.

Also, think about where you're going to park. If you've got a garage or driveway that's full of junk, clear it out: parking off road means cheaper premiums. Adding an alarm or immobiliser may also help lower the cost, whilst driving convictions like speeding or being caught holding a mobile whilst driving can send costs soaring.

Remember to only list your car at its current market value, not the price you paid for it. That's the amount insurers will pay out if the car is written off or stolen. The figure should come from industry price guides, like Glass's (glass.co.uk). To help ensure an accurate estimate, check out Which?'s car valuations calculator.

Other extras to add on or remove, depending on whether you want to boost peace of mind or to cut the cost, include:

- Protected no-claims – this will add up to fifteen per cent on top of your premium cost, but means even after a crash you'll still retain an NCD.

- Courtesy car – having an alternative vehicle in the event of a crash or theft may be crucial to some.

- Medical expenses – covers extras like physio if you developed whiplash after a crash.

- Personal belongings – insures those extras in the car like CDs, posh sunglasses, handbag etc.

- Driving other people's' cars.

A few minutes' twiddling with the excess can also boost cover at no extra cost: often a £300 and £250 excess will cost the same amount, so you may as well opt for the lower one. But don't increase your voluntary excess to an unaffordable level: however good a driver you think you are, not everyone else on the road is. Crashes happen, and if you need to make a claim you'll have to pay your voluntary excess on top of a compulsory one (often in place for drivers under the age of twenty-five, for example). Make sure you'd be able to afford it if an accident did happen.

Home insurance

Here there are two types: buildings insurance, which covers anything that could damage the structure of your home, like a fire, flooding or subsidence, and a contents policy, which insures everything inside. Buildings cover is normally a legal obligation for homeowners under the terms of a mortgage; contents insurance is optional and can be taken out by owners or renters.

Home cover is often haggle-friendly. So whilst it's well worth carrying out the above shopping around, and then working out what cashback you could get, before clicking 'buy' it's worth making a phone call or two to those offering the cheapest deal, and/or your current insurer. Ask if they can beat the deal you've found and, if you're buying both contents and building insurance, haggle. Many providers will offer a discount if you're buying both.

Make sure you're insuring only what you need. With buildings cover, don't mistake 'sum insured' for the amount that you'd put your home on the market for. Instead, it should be how much it would cost to rebuild if the whole place collapsed/burnt down/flooded/was blitzed by aliens from outer space/etc. Unless you're Bob the Builder, you won't find it easy to work out this amount – which should include materials, manpower, and somewhere for you to live in the meantime – but luckily there's a handy tool on the Association of British Insurers' website – abi.org.uk – which will help you find out.

As for contents, the most accurate way to work out the value you need to insure is just to walk through each room of your home and tot up the cost of replacing everything with new versions. You'll need to list expensive items – such as an engagement ring or valuable furniture – separately on the policy. Or you could opt for the easy – but less exact – method: L&G has a contents calculator on its site, legalandgeneral.com.

The one way you should never try to cut costs on home insurance is by becoming under-insured. Say you only took out contents cover for £15,000 worth of goods, but actually had possessions worth twice that, in the event of a claim, an insurer could either only pay out half the value of your belongings, or even cancel the whole policy. The same is true of a building policy: if you build an extension, that extra loft bedroom or conservatory will boost the value of your home and needs to be declared.

So how can you trim your bill? Don't assume you need all extras. Take legal expense cover, for instance. It could be useful, say if you needed legal advice in a dispute with a neighbour, but insurers say it's not used very often. Avoid 'double insuring' – if your iPhone is covered by a paid-for current account's mobile phone insurance policy, for example, don't include it on your home cover. Fitting a burglar alarm and five-cylinder lock, and joining a local neighbourhood watch scheme can also lower your quote. If you want to compare two policies on the same screen to ensure the quotes are like-for-like, visit find.co.uk/insurance/homes/compare-buildings.

Travel insurance

Again, there are two types: annual or single trip policies. Nearly everyone taking two trips or more a year will find an annual travel policy works out cheaper than a single visit one. But if you're booking one week in Spain over summer, a single policy – which will cost only a few quid if booked correctly – is all you will need.

The vast majority of travel insurance claims come from medical expenses and cancellation, so this should be your focus. In Europe and other developed countries apart from the US, most claims are under £500,000, but elsewhere over £1 million medical cover is important. Check the small print to make sure you're not paying too much or getting too little: many insurers, for example, include places like Morocco and Israel as part of Europe, so there's no need to opt for worldwide cover on a single policy if you're travelling to those countries.

Again, remember to avoid over-insuring: if you've covered your iPad as a single item including 'outside the home' cover on your home insurance, there's no need to include it in your travel policy too. But make sure your baggage allowance is enough to pay out for everything you're stuffed into your suitcase: the average single-article limit is £300, which wouldn't be enough to cover most laptops. Personal liability and legal expenses cover are extras that you might want to eliminate if you're trying to save money – they cover costs if you're sued, which you probably aren't protected against whilst at home.

To boost your protection abroad, apply for an EHIC – European Health Insurance Card – which gives you medical treatment if you fall ill or are injured in EU countries at a cheaper price or sometimes free. For more details and to apply, see ehic.org.uk.

To protect your purchase of the holiday, it's a good idea to pay for at least the deposit of your trip with a credit card, which will provide protection for the whole cost of the trip (see page 232) if the goods or services provided whilst you're away are not satisfactory. Also, anyone booking a package break through a holiday company that is a member of the Association of British Travel Agents will receive a refund if the operator goes bust (see page 76). If you're going down the DIY route, ensure your accommodation is booked via an ABTA travel agent and your flights via a provider which holds an Air Travel Organiser's Licence; that way, if either the airline or agent went into administration, your money would be refunded.

Ten money-saving rules

1. **Embrace the word 'free'.**
   You really can enjoy yourself for free. Whether it's
   a simple night in, reading (a book from the library,
   or one of the zillions of brilliant reads online, from
   newspapers to collected brilliance sites like jezebel.
   com, salon.com, postsecret.com and lettersofnote.
   com), or a free cinema preview, mystery-shopping
   dinner, board games night with friends, department
   store beauty makeover or park exercise session.

2. **'Can I afford it and is it worth it?' – stick these words
   on your credit cards.**
   And ask yourself these questions before buying
   anything, ever. No flashy car/laptop/diamond/etc. is
   worth the stress and sleepless nights that going into
   debt inevitably involves. If necessities are becoming
   a struggle to afford, see if rule six helps and seek
   professional advice. For luxuries, buy only when you can
   afford them, prioritising those you want most and . . .

3. **Make research routine.**
   Take a little time to research whatever you're buying,
   be it energy or a new TV. Mix your sources: for price,
   online comparison sites are hard to beat; for reliability
   and quality, ask friends, family, experts and social
   networking contacts. Building research into every

buying decision will help you secure the very best purchase every time.

4. Think value, not price.

Sometimes it's worth spending extra money to ensure you receive a reliable, long-lasting service from whatever you're buying, be it handyman, hoody or house. Think cost-per-use and factor in potential maintenance costs.

5. Sales can equal fail.

Be wary of anything that costs less than half its normal price – if it's on the sale rail at eighty per cent off, could it be faulty? If a house has had its asking price slashed, are there hidden structural problems? The buzzword is 'wary', not walk away – it could be a great deal, but make sure you know what you're letting yourself in for. Although, if it's a sharply reduced pair of neon leggings, it may be best just to walk away.

6. Do it yourself.

Embrace adversity as an opportunity to become more independent. Learn new practical skills – car maintenance, DIY, craft-making, accounting, sewing, plumbing, growing your own food. Sign up to a course or teach yourself with the help of handbooks and online videos and guides. And if getting greasy under the bonnet or bored working through a P60 feels dull, think how much you'll save over a lifetime and what you can spend that on.

7. Set a budget.

Force yourself to sit down and really work out what comes in each month, and what goes out again. Work out how best to use your money, and your long-term aims. If you've debts, work out a repayment plan (seek help from the sources listed below); if you've surplus, invest in a savings account, home, stocks or other non-under-the-mattress places. Budgeting software can be helpful: I like the simplicity of moflo.co.uk. Challenging yourself to shave off a certain amount from your monthly spending will help you avoid frittering away cash.

8. **Re-visit your budget.**
Regularly. If specific costs are rising, try to cut back elsewhere. Be in control of your spending. Use the review time to focus on the big costs – mortgage, energy bills, rented items – the largest expenses should be the most closely monitored ones. If cheaper deals are available, look at the merits of switching.

9. **Know when to buy . . .**
For train tickets, it's twelve weeks ahead. For holidays, it's months ahead or very last-minute. For fireplaces, it's summer; for oranges, it's winter. Know when is the best time to buy what you're buying, and, if applicable, stock up when the time is right.

10. **. . . and how to buy it.**
Protect yourself by buying expensive items on credit cards, from their cheapest source, and using the comparison-cashback combination that will help you earn yourself the largest savings – so you can enjoy ausperity living.

PART 5
Directory

SPENDING IT

Shopping

High street: free apps like RedLaser and Shoparazzi help to work out if deals are decent

Reward cards: Tesco Clubcard: tesco.com/clubcard; Boots Advantage Card: boots.com/en/Advantage-Card; Nectar: nectar.com; Superdrug Beautycard: superdrug.com/page/beautycard

Deal alerts: lovefashionsales.com

Student discounts: On computer software: http://viglen.software2. co.uk; Apple goods: store.apple.com/uk/browse/home/ education_routing. Range of shops and online: National Union of Students Extra Card: nus.org.uk/en/nus-extra

Charity shops in London: timeout.com/london/shopping/ features/2503/London-s_best_charity_shops.html

Discount and outlet stores: TK Maxx: tkmaxx.com; McArthur Glen chain: mcarthurglen.com; Bicester Village in Oxfordshire: bicestervillage.com; Clarks Village: clarksvillage.co.uk

Online shopping: Price comparison sites: kelkoo.co.uk, priceinspector.co.uk, smartshopping.co.uk, pricerunner.co.uk or Google Shopping: google.co.uk/shopping

Cashback: topcashback.co.uk, quidco.com, greasypalm.co.uk

Compare cashback amounts: moneysavingexpert.com/shopping/ cashback-sites-comparison

Voucher sites: myvouchercodes.co.uk, discountvouchers.co.uk

Amazon discounts: zeezaw.co.uk, pricecutreview.com/UK

eBay discounts: fatfingers.co.uk, and 'sniper' auctionstealer.co.uk

Group buying: groupon.co.uk, wowcher.com, kelkooselect.co.uk, keynoir.com, livingsocial.com, wahanda.com

Buying the big stuff

Lower-power household devices: energysavingtrust.org.uk/In-your-home/Products-for-your-home

Cars: Advice from car-selling site motors.co.uk; check log books with the DVLA on 0300 790 6802

Weddings

Budgets: google.com/weddings/plan.html, hitched.co.uk whimsicalwonderlandweddings.com/2011/01/wedding-budget-planner-list.html

The dress: stillwhite.co.uk, preloved.co.uk and sellmyweddingdress. co.uk; oxfam.org.uk/shop/bridal

Sample sales: bridesmagazine.co.uk/events

Invites: weddingchicks.com/freebies, smilebox.com/wedding-invitations.html, vistaprint.co.uk, paperlesspost.com

Insurance: moneysupermarket.com/wedding-insurance

Christmas

Food: lovefoodhatewaste.com, hotukdeals.com

Presents (budget for them): debtadvicefoundation.org/debt-tools/present-planner

Home-made ideas: knitting: watchknitting.com; make gift vouchers: giftcertificatefactory.com, one4allgiftcard.co.uk

Unusual present ideas: etsy.com, notonthehighstreet.com

Cards: theworks.co.uk, Hobbycraft: hobbycraft.co.uk

Holidays

Hotels: compare prices with tripadvisor.com, hotels.com, expedia. co.uk, booking.com, thomascook.com, otel.com, venere.com, trivago.co.uk and travelsupermarket.com

Secret hotel rooms: hotwire.com and lastminute.com. Identify them at secrethotelsrevealed.co.uk and tinyurl.com/MSEsecret

Hostels: oops-paris.com, snowdoniahostel.co.uk, kadirstreehouses. com; aggregator sites: hostelbooks.com and hostelworld.com

Holiday homes: holidaylettings.co.uk (more than 50,000 holiday homes in 116 countries), holiday-rentals.co.uk (300,000 self-catering cottages, apartments and villas) and ownersdirect.co.uk (33,000)

ABTA guarantee: abta.com/consumer-services

Check out homes at maps.google.com; pay using paypal.co.uk

Package breaks: travelsupermarket.com, travelzoo.co.uk and teletextholidays.co.uk

House swap: homeforexchange.com and homelink.org.uk;

guardianhomeexchange.co.uk; the National Childbirth Trust's ncthouseswap.ning.com; sabbaticalhomes.com matches up academics; swapmycitypad.com offers professional networks

Couch-surfing: airbnb.com, couchsurfing.org, wheretosleep.co.uk, crashpadder.com

Camping and 'garden surfing': campinmygarden.com, find-a-campsite.co.uk, coolcamping.co.uk

Flight comparison sites: momondo.com, kayak.co.uk, travelocity.co.uk, travelsupermarket.com, skyscanner.net

Charter flights: charterflights.co.uk.

Secret flights: lastminute.com/site/travel/flights/deals/top-secret.html

Wear your luggage: jaktogo.com, cabinmaxluggage.co.uk

Ferry: aggregator sites such as ferrysavers.com or aferry.co.uk

Train: comprehensive rail info: seat61.com. European trains – France: tgv-europe.com; Switzerland: sbb.ch; Italy: trenitalia.com; Germany: bahn.de; Austria: oebb.at; Spain: renfe.com; Portugal: cp.pt; Sweden: sj.se; Czech Republic: cd.cz/eshop

International train services: Eurostar: eurostar.com; Thalys, high-speed trains Paris-Brussels-Amsterdam & Cologne: thalys.com; Thello, sleeper train from Paris to Milan, Verona and Venice: thello.com; City Night Line sleeper trains from Paris to Berlin, Munich and Hamburg, and from Amsterdam to Zurich, Munich, Prague, Copenhagen and Warsaw via bahn.de

Holiday money: track exchange rates: travelex.co.uk/uk/personal/ratetracker.aspx; compare rates: travelmoneymax.com

Car hire (compare deals): moneymaxim.co.uk and carrentals.co.uk

Stand-alone excess-protection policies: protectyourbubble.com, questor-insurance.co.uk, carhireexcess.com

Cycling abroad: European bike routes: eurovelo.org

Cheap ski kit rental: alpinresorts.com

Be paid to travel and work abroad: anyworkanywhere.com, schemes include Bunac: bunac.org/uk

Disney deals: mousesavers.com

Insider knowledge and deals on holidays: jetsetter.com

Nightlife (and day trips)

Look up drinks and bar/club prices in London: designmynight.com

Theatre tickets comparison sites: comparetheatretickets.com, seatchoice.com, theatrebillboard.com, theatremonkey.com

Agencies to compare prices: ticketmaster.co.uk, ticketline.co.uk, stargreen.com

Fan ticket sites: viagogo.co.uk and seatwave.com

Classified ticket websites: gumtree.com

Theatre deals: lastminute.com; £5 tickets at shakespearesglobe.com; National Theatre in London: nationaltheatre.org.uk; half-price ticket booth: tkts.co.uk

Watch TV shows filmed: sroaudiences.com, applausestore.com, bbc.co.uk/showsandtours/tickets, bbc.co.uk/showsandtours/beonashow

Listings sites: timeout.com/London; 'view' followed by the nameofthetown.co.uk such as viewbath.co.uk for Bath, Belfast, Birmingham, Bournemouth, Bradford, Brighton, Bristol, Cambridge, Cardiff, Edinburgh, Glasgow, Hull, Leeds, Leicester, Liverpool, London, Manchester, Nottingham, Oxford and Sheffield

Free attendance at summer music festivals by volunteering: see the likes of oxfam.org.uk/stewarding

Horse-racing days out: britishracecourses.org

England football fans club for reduced tickets: http://englandfans.thefa.com

Tennis ballot for Wimbledon tickets: via tennis clubs at lta.org.uk or call 020 8487 7000, or send a stamped addressed envelope to AELTC, PO Box 98, London SW19 5AE between August and December

Free film previews: seefilmfirst.com and momentumpictures.co.uk

Free Orange sim card for Orange Wednesdays: freesim.orange.co.uk

Exercise

Free gym passes: fitnessfirst.co.uk/weekjanuary, lafitness.co.uk, nuffieldhealth.com, esporta.com, virginactive.co.uk. Cheap day passes: payasugym.com

No-frills gyms: thegymgroup.com, puregym.com, fitspacegyms.co.uk

Free sessions: British Military Fitness: britmilfit.com; curves.co.uk (women only)

Free, at-home fitness ideas: exercise.com

MILKING IT

Food and booze

Use-by dates: fsis.usda.gov

Leftover ideas: lovefoodhatewaste.com, supercook.com and allrecipes.com

Supermarket comparison site: mysupermarket.com

Supermarket and other shopping offers: fixtureferrets.co.uk, hotukdeals.com

Own-brands reviews: supermarketownbrandguide.co.uk

Butcher locator: findabutcher.co.uk

Discount stores and cash and carries: aldi.co.uk, lidl.co.uk, costco. co.uk, booker.co.uk, store.makro.co.uk

Bargain food near the end of its shelf life: approvedfood.co.uk

Alcohol deals: quaffersoffers.co.uk

Restaurant offers: vouchercode.co.uk, moneysavingexpert. com/deals/cheap-restaurant-deals. For smartphone users: vouchercloud.com app, toptable.co.uk and 5pm.co.uk

Restaurant membership cards: gourmetsociety.co.uk, tastecard.co.uk

BYOB restaurants, including details of corkage fees: wine-pages. com/food/byoblist.shtml

Grow your own: kitchengardeners.org, *How to Grow Your Food – A Guide for Complete Beginners* by Jon Clift and Amanda Cuthbert (Green Books, £5.99)

Clothes

Learn how to make do and mend: sewing.org/html/guidelines.html

Do your own dry-cleaning: tinyurl.com/beckmannkit and tinyurl. com/hagertykit

Hundreds of ideas for making your own clothes: threadbanger.com (with videos)

Video site that tells you how to do nearly everything: videojug.com

Home

Furniture: make others' cast-offs your own at uk.freecycle.org

Bargain property ideas: homesandbargains.co.uk, alisonathome. co.uk

Furniture sales outlets: homebrands.co.uk, londonwarehouse.co.uk, trade-secret.co.uk

Latest home retailers' clearance deals: homesandbargains.co.uk/
sales-and-vouchers

Charity furniture shops: tinyurl.com/redcrossfurniture, oxfam.org.
uk/shops/content/furniture.html, salvationarmy.org.uk/uki/
shops, emmaus.org.uk/find and emmaus.org.uk/shops/ebay

Designer-quality furniture: made.com, milandirect.co.uk

Fabrics and wallpaper: top-designer.co.uk, kingdominteriors.co.uk,
curtainfactoryoutlet.co.uk, looseendsfabrics.co.uk

Bathrooms: screwfix.com, betterbathrooms.com, heatandplumb.
com, Rotherhithe-based F.E.E.T International: feet-international.
co.uk

Kitchens: kdcuk.co.uk – imported German, high-gloss kitchens at a
discount; paragonfuniture.co.uk has bespoke wood carpentry; for
granite worktops: greekmarbles.com

Replace door handles or doors rather than whole new set of
cupboards: Homestyle (doors.homestylekitchens.co.uk, 0871
2227845)

Accessories: designer door handles: handleworld.co.uk; cushions:
cushionsonline.co.uk; cushioncouture.co.uk; dunelm-mill.co.uk;
matalan.co.uk; wilkinsonplus.co.uk

Replacing parts of crockery, glass and cutlery sets:
chinapresentations.net, chinasearch.co.uk

Building work: tradesman recommendation sites: ratedpeople.com,
myhammer.co.uk

Cleaning: old-school tips at vinegartips.com; howtocleananything.
com

Reclaim council tax: the Valuation Office Agency's website at voa.
gov.uk and 0845 602 1507

Inchbald School of Design: inchbald.co.uk

Beauty

Spa deals and beauty discounts: wahanda.com

Free and cheap lotions and deals: moneysavingexpert.com/deals/
cheap-free-beauty-deals

Kitchen-cupboard cosmetics: makeyourcosmetics.com

Beauty reviews (work out if creams and lotions actually work):
makeupalley.com/product

Cheap make-up: eyeslipsface.co.uk; strawberrynet.com; feelunique.
com

Quoted beauty advice: The Lanes Health and Beauty:

thelaneshealthandbeauty.com; salon group Cannelle:
cannellebeaute.com

Swap-it shop

Clothes: rent at girlmeetsdress.com, onenightstand.co.uk,
   wishwantwear.com, bigwardrobe.com. Real-world swaps: swishing.
   org, mrsbears.co.uk, swapstyle.com and rehashclothes.com
Books: bookmooch.com, readitswapit.co.uk
Skills: swapaskill.com, skillsbox.com
Tickets: swapmyticket.co.uk
Bags: myhandbagswap.com

Transport

Cheaper fuel: petrolprices.com
Reputable garages/reviews: honestjohn.co.uk
Second-hand parts: autopartstrader.co.uk
Learn car maintenance: haynes.co.uk, tinyurl.com/carmaintain
Plan train journeys in advance: nationalrail.co.uk/times_fares/
   booking_horizons.html; Cheap ticket alerts: thetrainline.com/
   ticketalert
Find route operators: nationalrail.co.uk.
Cheap deals via Megatrain: uk.megabus.com
Rail booking sites: thetrainline.com, raileasy.co.uk
Journey-splitting: splityourticket.co.uk
Railcards: railcard.co.uk; disabled railcard eligibility: tinyurl.com/
   disabledelig
Season ticket costs: ojp.nationalrail.co.uk/service/seasonticket/
   search
Train journey refunds: trainrefunds.co.uk, or on the London Tube:
   tfl.gov.uk/tfl/tickets/refunds/tuberefund
Cycling savings: cycletoworkcalculator.com
Government bike-buying scheme with tax benefits: cyclescheme.
   co.uk/getting-a-bike or 0844 879 5105
Register your bike's frame number with the police: immobilise.com
Free cycling training: cycletraining.co.uk
Bike insurance comparison site: moneysupermarket.com/home-
   insurance/bicycle-insurance
Walk (find the most direct or pleasant route): walkit.com
Cut moving costs: shiply.com (online marketplace for goods
   transport)

MAKING IT

Money-making

Rent-your-stuff sites: rentmyitems.com, uk.zilok.com

Rent a room: spareroom.co.uk, uk.easyroommate.com, mondaytofriday.com

Tax advice on the rent-a-room scheme: hmrc.gov.uk/individuals/tmarent-a-room-scheme.shtml

Rent your driveway: parkatmyhouse.com

Rent your car: blablacar.com, liftshare.com, whipcar.com

Rent your spare space: storemates.co.uk or sharemystorage.com

Rent your garden: campinmygarden.com

Turn your home into a movie set: locationworks.com, lavishlocations.com, amazingspace.co.uk, location-collective.co.uk. Or contact production companies direct.

Sell on eBay: ebay.com, get4it.co.uk

Sell electrical items: mazumamobile.com, tescomobilerecycle.com; high street chain Cex: find a branch at uk.webuy.com/stores. Or compare rates at moneysavingexpert.com/phones/mobile-recycling

Sell books: find your local second-hand book store or visit amazon.co.uk/marketplace or greenmetropolis.com

Brainiac money-makers: Any Question Answered jobs: aqa.63336.com/vacancies.htm, solve science problems for cash: innocentive.com

Paid-survey sites: yougov.com, valuedopinions.co.uk, globaltestmarket.com, uk.toluna.com, panelbase.net

Focus groups: sarosresearch.com, indiefield.net, the Grapevine Panel from fieldinitiatives.co.uk, focus4people.com, focusforce.net and claret-uk.com

Earn from your own website: google.co.uk/adsense, affiliate-program.amazon.co.uk

Sell your photos: istockphoto.com, alamy.com, crestock.com

Sell your story: contact newspapers and magazines direct, or use an agency like featureworld.co.uk, or talktothepress.co.uk

Sell your talents: fivesquids.co.uk, etsy.com, peopleperhour.com, freelancer.com or studentgems.com

Ask your boss for a pay rise: I don't have his/her contact details though, sorry!

Check your tax code: hmrc.gov.uk/calcs/stc.htm

Find lost money: mylostaccount.org.uk, thepensionservice.gov.uk, or investmentuk.org

Mystery shopping: retaileyes.co.uk, amberarch.com, gapbuster.com/mystery-shopping, tnsglobal.com, grassrootsmysteryshopping.com, bareinternational.com and retail-maxim.co.uk. For people aged twenty-five and under: oldenoughtodrink.co.uk

Sell door to door or host parties. Ann Summers: annsummers.com; The Body Shop: thebodyshop.co.uk; Jamie Oliver at Home: jamieathome.com/lets-party.html; Colour Me Beautiful cosmetics: colourmebeautiful.co.uk, Pampered Chef: pamperedchef.co.uk/join_us/menu_opp.html; Avon: avon.uk.com

Sell old print cartridges: cashforcartridges.co.uk, inkcycle.co.uk

Tax check-up: hmrc.gov.uk/selfemployed

FINANCIAL STUFF

Banking

Mortgages: compare options at money.co.uk/mortgages.htm; Which? Guide to Mortgages: tinyurl.com/whichmortgages

Financial services money-saving, including updated guides to top buys: moneysavingexpert.com

Debt advice: Consumer Credit Counselling Service: cccs.co.uk or contactus@cccs.co.uk or 0800 138 1111; nationaldebtline.co.uk or 0808 808 4000; Citizens Advice Bureau: citizensadvice.org.uk or call 08444 111 444 in England or 08444 77 20 20 in Wales; Debtors Anonymous: debtorsanonymous.org.uk or 020 7117 7533

Benefits advice: disability advice before you have made a claim: 0800 882 200 or textphone 0800 24 33 55. Once you've made a claim: 08457 123 456 or textphone 08457 22 44 33. Child Support Agency national helpline: 08457 133 133 or textphone 08457 138 924

Credit cards: view top balance transfer deals: tinyurl.com/MSEbalancetransfers; moneyfacts.co.uk

Sample Consumer Credit Act claim letters: which.co.uk/consumer-rights/sale-of-goods/understanding-the-consumer-credit-act/sample-letters

Trading Standards: to find your local office visit tradingstandards.gov.uk or contact your local council

'Soft search' for a new credit card: moneysupermarket.com/credit-cards

Check credit rating (go via a cashback website): experian.co.uk or 0844 481 8000, equifax.co.uk

Savings: most generous savings deals: moneynet.co.uk, moneyfacts.co.uk.

Financial Services Compensation Scheme: fscs.org.uk or 0800 678 1100

Advice Guide (from Citizens Advice): help with debt, benefits, housing rights, consumer problems: adviceguide.org.uk or 08454 04 05 06

Retirement advice: direct.gov.uk/en/pensionsandretirementplanning/index.htm, pensionsadvisoryservice.org.uk

Compensation: sample PPI complaint letters: which.co.uk/campaigns/personal-finance/the-ppi-campaign/claim-back

Financial Ombudsman service: financial-ombudsman.org.uk, 0800 023 4567

Pensions Protection Fund: 0845 600 2541 or pensionsprotectionfund.org.uk

To find an independent financial advisor: unbiased.co.uk

Phones

Compare home-phone providers: homephonechoices.co.uk

Bundles including satellite TV: simplifydigital.co.uk; free helpline 0800 542 4704

Avoid expensive phone numbers: saynoto0870.com

Never phone abroad without an access code: niftylist.co.uk/calls

Free online telephony site: skype.com, vbuzzer.com or google.com/voice. Some, including Skype, also have an app so you can phone international numbers for nothing, or at a low price, from your mobile

Mobiles (analyse usage and compare tariffs): billmonitor.com, omio.com, moneysupermarket.com, onecompare.com

Energy

Comparison services: energyhelpline.com (or 0800 074 0745), uswitch.com (or 0800 051 5493 for a postal service), simplyswitch.com, ukpower.co.uk

Lazy route to switching: incahoot.com/concierge

Loft insulation: free from energy suppliers (contact yours) or for installation: nationalinsulationassociation.org.uk/housholder

Energy grants: energysavingtrust.org.uk/Take-action/Grants-and-Discounts-Database

Advice: Energy Saving Trust: in England, Wales or Northern Ireland call 0300 123 1234, in Scotland call 0800 512 012 or energysavingtrust.org.uk; centralheating.co.uk

Energy-saving devices: large range available via the Energy Saving Trust (see above), also ecoflap.co.uk, chimneyballoon.co.uk, eco-button.com

Water: find out if a meter would save you money at ccwater.org.uk

Gas Safe Register: gassaferegister.co.uk

Insurance

Comparison sites: moneysupermarket.com, confused.com, comparethemarket.com, gocompare.com

Motor: car valuations calculator at which.co.uk/cars/choosing-a-car/buying-a-car/car-valuations

Home value calculator: abi.org.uk

Home contents calculator: tinyurl.com/contentscalc

Compare policies side by side: find.co.uk/insurance/homes/compare-buildings

Travel: European Health Insurance Card: ehic.org.uk

Index

**Join the AUSPERITY movement –
it's the lifestyle choice sweeping the nation!**

Find an online directory of all the websites recommended
in this book and access FREE ADDED CONTENT –
videos, blog posts and more – by visiting:

ausperity.com *

Find out more: **@lucytobin**
Join the conversation: **#Ausperity**
lucytobin.com

HERON
B O O K S

heronbooks.co.uk

* The side-effects of ausperity may include a bloated bank account
and an enhanced quality of life.